MW00636542

MUDFLAP

THE GLOVES COME OFF

JAY ALDEN BAILEY

575 Main Street Press
New Hartford, Connecticut

Copyright © 2020 by Jay Alden Bailey

Notice of Rights

All rights reserved. No part of this book may be reproduced in any form or by any electronic or mechanical means, including information storage and retrieval systems – except in the case of brief quotations embodied in critical articles or reviews – without permission in writing from the author.

Disclaimer

This is a work of creative nonfiction. The events are portrayed to the best of Jay Alden Bailey's memory. While all the stories in the book are true, the names have been changed to protect the privacy of the people involved.

Library of Congress Control Number: 2020920716

Publisher's Cataloging-In-Publication Data

Names: Bailey, Jay Alden, author.
Title: Mudflap: The Gloves Come Off. [Book 2] / Jay Alden Bailey
Description: New Hartford, CT: 575 Main Street Press, [2020]
Identifiers: ISBN 9781733746533 (paperback) ISBN 9781733746540 (ebook)
Subjects: LCSH: Bailey, Jay Alden—Humor. | United States—Social conditions—1945—Humor. | United States—Economic conditions—1945—Humor. | Selflessness (Psychology)—Humor. | American wit and humor. |Social satire. | LCGFT: Humor.

ISBN-13: 978-1-7337465-3-3

Published by 575 Main Street Press
P.O. Box 496
New Hartford, Connecticut 06057
Telephone: (860) 830-4398
www.mudflapthehero.com

Dedicated to:

My Sweet Wife Martha
who would never bully anyone.

TABLE OF CONTENTS

Quote: From Historians throughout history.

"If we choose to forget we are destined to repeat."

Mudflap was excited as he wrapped up his first book. When every last detail was finished and ready to print, he gave a huge sigh of relief and turned off the computer.

As he stood up and watched the screen go dark, he felt an emptiness that he did not expect or like, not one little bit at all.

Mudflap had more fish to fry.

Author's Note

I want to take you on a journey:

The book starts with some personal perspectives and anecdotes from local experiences, then it pushes ideas and enlightenments into the national, global and universal realms.

Some of the content is heavy and I didn't want to make it an academic bore. So, I have tried to keep it light with a lot of dry humor for your entertainment, and make it all relatable, too.

Big change starts small within us all.

Jay Alden Bailey

Preface

You may or may not agree with the way this particular Mudflap reacts to the world around him. You might applaud and or laugh. You could cringe and feel disdain. Everyone will take away many different things.

In the first book you got to know Mudflap, who he is and the battles he faced without much guidance. This time, he's here to inspire you again with more anecdotes and philosophical insights.

Looking for positive influences without seeing everything through a rose-colored filter, Mudflap will share experiences about a variety of people at many levels, who come at you from all sorts of different angles and perspectives.

If there's one thing to be learned along the way, it is to avoid the negative energies from self-serving people who don't have your best interest in mind.

Stay focused on your goals regardless of how others try to discourage you. Embrace the positive-energy people in your life and continue to attract more like them.

If you change one of your opinions or are inspired to do better in any way, the book's purpose will have been achieved.

P.S. Real Time: This is an addition to chapters and segments; it refers to what's happening in our fast-paced world as the author edits and finishes the book.

INTRODUCTION

A Mudflap is any person who puts their own interest below that of another person or a cause.

Human nature is to view the world from a personal perspective, it's a basic knee-jerk reaction.

Looking through someone else's eyes requires a bit more thought and reflection.

Agreeing with someone with whom we disagree can be a humbling experience, but the change, an enlightenment not anticipated, is a growth spurt for our souls.

In the first book, Mudflap said many direct things and others were more implied. He tip-toed around some issues but not this time. The gloves come off!

If you're looking for Flowery-Described Scenes, Bunnies, Unicorns and Stardust, you're reading the wrong book.

The Mudflap Poem

You could be a hero at first, then a villain the next,
what the future holds we do not know.

Keep your karma clean and watch your step
or "under the bus" you go.

MF. > Out !

Prologue

Mudflap was attending a CAPA meeting. (Connecticut Authors and Publishers Association) He was in a conversation with a Publisher who was extremely conservative, and the subject of "summer reads" came up.

Without thinking it through, Mudflap said, "I read Michelle Obama's book *Becoming*.

The Publisher snapped at him and exclaimed, "Why would you read that crap?"

Mudflap replied, "Well, first of all, she is an historic figure being the first and only African-American First Lady. And secondly, how does anyone learn anything if they are only exposed to people who are like them, agree all the time, and never get another person's perspective?"

He emphasized, "Do you just want to hear echoes and listen to yes Ma'am all the time?"

Mudflap went on, "Every once in a while, you should switch the channel to MSNBC and listen to what the other side is saying. They both tell you only what they want you to hear, always focused on half the truth, and conveniently leaving out many additional facts. If you pay attention to both sides, the real truth is somewhere in the middle, a combination of both."

The Bully

"Bullies are scared people hiding inside scary people."

Bullies are nothing new. They have been a part of life from the beginning: a survival-of-the-fittest emotion born from the need to provide and dominate. A mentality ingrained deep into our primordial psyche.

The evolved mind understands that there is a clash of wills among different peoples; the primitive mind interprets that clash as a need to be a bully.

The evolved repress anger, greed, jealousy, and other negative emotions; the primitive is fueled by these emotions.

Bullies have finally been called out in our schools and work places. Now they saturate the internet and every venue we can think of; bullies surround us influencing our lives whether we like it or not.

They are everywhere and should be avoided, but sometimes you can't and they must be called out and confronted.

Bullies are in vogue in our world leadership. Russia, China, and Brazil are the most recognizable; these influential leaders we as a nation must confront. The Battle Grounds are in order as listed: Defense, Trade, and the Environment.

Like Stalin standing up to Hitler, one bully defying another, we picked our own bully to stand fast up against the strongmen of our adversaries.

America has been sick of partisan politics for as long as any of us can remember. The common person is helpless against our elected leaders, who we watch, cycle after cycle, squabble, bicker and not get enough done for us in the process. We are bullied by our own leadership and struggle through the fog they create to see what's really true and best for our future.

Allies like Britain have picked their own strongman, too, keeping pace with the others.

Mudflap is not extreme right or left, and is not making judgments, only observations. The judgments are the readers to make.

We have big bullies on the top and an assortment of little bullies and pests all the way down through the ranks of life, business, and social situations alike.

The reality is most people fall into the middle of the issues and are left dealing with the extremists of our society.

The only true common denominator is one thing: we all desire to be happy in one way or another.

Mudflap's aim is only to help bring some sanity to an ever increasingly crazy world.

Round II

THE GLOVES COME OFF

Mudflaps catch the dirt, grime, and debris from the road of life, protecting the people and causes they care about.

The only difference between a Mudflap and a Doormat is that a Mudflap is vertical and bolted down, not horizontal or easy to move out of the way.

Stay on your feet and don't let them walk all over you. Mudflap, Over and Out !

Mudflap likes history; it's filled with heroes, villains, and lessons that should not be forgotten.

Herman Melville's *Moby-Dick* is a great example of a deep philosophical read that has relevant messages that span the distance of time.

Moby-Dick hits on many issues and themes, like obsession, revenge, and redemption. The layers of messages and story-line morals run so deep that they reach different people at all sorts of levels and perspectives.

In his egotistical madness to pursue a monster, Ahab, the righteous, took everybody down with him. But the whale was not really the demon, he was just standing up for all the other whales.

Who really was the possessed?

Melville was a prophet of sorts, warning us of leaders, like Hitler, whose obsessions not only drag down their own country, but take the world with them, too.

How about this: Does Ahab represent Man's leaders and Moby Dick the Earth?

Something to think about.
Mudflap, Over and Out

Chapter 1

The Literary World

Literal Bullies
You can be crazy as long as you're nice

Publishers
Sorry about the shipping costs, but I'm not Amazon.

Literary Censorship
The Power of the Pout
Censorship in the form of Snobbery

History vs. Science Fiction
1984 The Book by George Orwell
The Book Burners were an extreme version of censorship, but not unique.

The Nazis burned books.

Jay Alden Bailey

The Ancient Library of Alexandria was burned, too! Unimaginable what we lost.

Libraries and Knowledge Fight Tyranny Mudflap, Over and Out !

C all me Mudflap.

When writing the first book, it was easy to know where to start; it was in the beginning. The authors of the Bible had the same advantage, too; they started with nothing and then there was light.

The book *Mudflap* was an introduction. I will do the best I can to make this book stand alone. There are so many places and issues I want to address and tie in. Let me start you from a different beginning, my changing perspectives and experiences after writing the first book.

As a novice author, Mudflap was bumbling through the process of writing, editing and publishing. He learned a lot along the way, exposing himself to all different sorts of people whom he had never interacted with before.

Some were very gracious and surprisingly helpful; other's more shockingly rude and were obstructionists. Goes to show "you never know" who's really on your side.

If you think the conservative right is exclusionary, get a belly full of the extreme liberal left in the literary world and you will really get a stomachache.

Mudflap likes Connecticut and defends it against the reputation that it's a cold and callous place to live -- skeptical and private is more accurate. Mudflap is used to the aloof behavior of the state's residents, but he really got a shock himself at the demeanor of the publishers he encountered. He wanted to keep his business local and in state, so like the rest of the world today, he first tried the publishers he found online.

Wow, what a group! Mudflap found them to be the most condescending, snooty, rude and dismissive bunch he had ever yet dealt with, the absolute worst Connecticut has to offer. Most didn't return the calls and a high percentage listed had disconnected phone numbers. Out of the ones that did reply, only one was polite and gave him the time of day.

Talk about some sticks in the mud, what a tough crowd!

When going to the big publishers in New York you can just plain forget it. The bullies were in complete unison like a seasoned dance group with choreographed steps so completely in tune with each other that they were as one.

It's pitiful to be a new author trying to get help. You must have an agent to do business with the publishers. It's required. Then the agents don't call you back or even give you a courtesy reply to an email. They were the 2nd line of bullies excluding you from even getting a start.

Next, he looked into Author House and I Universe Publishers who say they help start-up authors. First of all, I think they are owned by the same group so it's no difference.

Mudflap got involved in contract with I Universe who, after they reviewed his files, wanted all sorts of additional releases not in the original contract. Mudflap explained he had gone to the Library of Congress and the Patent and Trademark Office personally, and the whole point of writing the book was to have the rights to the character idea and the visual art logo. The supervisor understood his position and said he would refund the card.

But somewhere up the chain of command they decided to bully him, steal his ideas and "logo".

When Mudflap fought back, argued about the additional releases and stood his ground, they bullied him some more by not only refusing to refund his card for the $1,000 deposit, they also refused to release the card form the additional fees that they expected to get in the future.

The giant publishing company I Universe needed to steal from the poor start-up author.

Then the credit card company was going to side with I Universe, and the two giant corporations decided to gang up on the financially poor, struggling, naive and ignorant little author.

They had the bank card, the credit score, the book files, and a contract they were breaching demanding that Mudflap had to pay anyway.

They thought they had Mudflap cold.

He was a lot bigger adversary than they thought. Mudflap had played hard ball with banks and lawyers before.

He was under the impression that your credit card gave you some degree of protection against bad or fraudulent transactions. It was shocking how fast they sided with the big company and how little they cared. Not only were they "not" going to cancel the original payment, they were going to continue to let the publisher take the additional three installments for services never rendered. They said, "You signed a contract, it's too bad, tough luck." The fact that the publisher wanted multiple additional releases not originally stated was of no consequence to the bank.

The big bank said, "We are not lawyers. Take them to court if you got a problem."

Mudflap replied, "If you're not lawyers, why then are you making a decision about the validity of the contract? They can take me to court if they don't like it."

Mudflap had to write up a long and detailed defense for the bank's review. Everything had to be completely spelled out in a redundant fashion. Mudflap, having played hard ball before, and unafraid of bully threats, made an additional thing very clear to the bank: if they decided to side with the other big company against him, he was going to cancel the card, and they could pound sand and eat the money they intended to release.

It took two months for the bank's legal department to make a decision.

Wisely, the bank sided in Mudflap's favor and the two big bullies backed off.

Coincidentally, (if you read the 1st book you know how Mudflap feels about coincidence), he met an author at the library who told him about an organization called CAPA, (Connecticut Authors and Publishers Association) and Mudflap found a home.

They were just the opposite of what he encountered with the first publishers he interacted with. The whole group were the most gracious and supportive people he had ever had the pleasure to deal with. They are almost too free with their time; a great example that Connecticut business-wise is an accepting place, giving people a chance based on ability and merit.

Mudflap's mom was a walking, talking dictionary, often shrieking and screaming, too. She loved nothing better than to throw a word out at you that you had never heard before (especially when she was mad) and tell you to look it up.

Her deep-rooted, Irish-Catholic upbringing gave her an extremely condescending tone when she got irritated. A sharp tongue so quick to strike, your head would spin. Mudflap watched many times as people fell quickly in the wake of her wrath. Slight in stature and most pleasant at first, she could take down any who dared cross or intimidate her. And bully her? Oh, God no! She was like having a little shield with you. Probably the most secure feeling for a kid was having her at your side when in any uncomfortable situation.

Mudflap's mom was an advocate for books of all kinds and she loved libraries, like she loved words. She had no problem tuning out the world with her nose deep in her read. The house was piled with books. The shelves attached to the walls had dramatic swooping bends from the weight of tightly packed rows. For people who didn't have a lot of material things, she and her new husband had a lot of money invested in books. Hard to imagine why with them being free at the library. She clearly had her favorites that she had to have and signed every one of them. Each one especially dated and endorsed in the beginning with comments and sayings to commemorate birthdays and holidays. Mudflap has a tiny bit of her library left in his rec room, on a specially designated table for her endorsed books only.

For this reason, Mudflap donated to his local library that was only partially funded by the town. He couldn't give them much because with a young family and small business there was never enough money. So, the library became a monthly bill, paying enough to push him up to a minimum of a $1,000 a year and his wife became a BookFriend, too, giving her time.

When Mudflap finished his first book, he was excited to bring it to the library, elated!

But his happiness was immediately crushed by the countenance of the first librarian he encountered. She gave a look as if she had just smelled something bad and was about to get nauseous. An old friend from this particular library who did the purchasing did graciously buy a book. A long-time library supporter and English teacher, too, took out the book and said he liked it and that it was good.

But Mudflap was getting some weird vibes from the rest of the crowd.

Who was he, some tree guy, some poor uneducated fool who dared to think he was an author? Mudflap felt a sting he really didn't like at all.

Wife is a bit of a literary snob herself and had been rolling her eyes from the start, and throughout the whole process of Mudflap's writing and editing. She rolled her eyes all the way to the Library of Congress and to the Patent and Trademark Office. She only started to come around after the Supervisor Lady who came out to help them liked and connected with Mudflap's character idea.

Librarians are the grunts of the literary world doing the hands-on chores kinda like the tree industry's ground-men/ground-persons.

Jay Alden Bailey

Ever notice when you add "persons" to any position it really means women?

Librarians see so many books they get numb. Just like Tree Guys who see wood all the time and disregard grain patterns in the pieces they cut. Then somebody who is a laymen/layperson comes along and says, "Wow, look at that cool grain. That would make a great table." The Tree Guy looks at them and rolls his eyes and may say something patronizing.

Books are like pieces of wood to a librarian, each just another one of many to be shuffled and sorted.

And self-published books are garbage, that's their first impression. Mudflap found this fact out directly from one of his clients who is a librarian at one of the local state colleges. Quote: "Self-published books are all crap. The authors are lucky to sell 200 at most and that's a stretch". She reluctantly purchased Mudflap's 1st book out of obligation and friendship. She has not been able to get into it, citing at first that it didn't have enough flowery described scenes, and it has just too much personal interaction.

So, for my Literary Snob of a friend I write a quick blurb:
Mudflap stepped outside into the fresh, sweet, morning air. Thousands of dewdrops glistened off the blades of grass, illuminated by the morning sunrise like stars in a galaxy. It was a moment of brief calm broken by more stars flashing through his head like a storm of little comets as his brother snapped him out of it with a punch upside the head.

There you go, Joan. That one's for you.
Mudflap, Over and Out !

Literary Bullies Crossing Lines

Business and Politics

Out of State and into Vacationland

Nothing like a Mean Librarian to Help You

Enjoy Your Summer Read
Mudflap, Over and Out !

Mudflap didn't want to show his work to a publisher before he printed his own first edition. He wanted the copyright and trademark work done first, then he would expose his ideas to the open market. As a seasoned businessman first and an author second, he was wary of trusting a publisher.

The literary and music world is full of plagiarism. Mudflap was not going to beg to be published, then dismissed, and in the end ripped off. He was on his game.

He was accused of paranoia by the eye rollers. Some librarians even snickered and smirked, saying, "You're too worried about nothing. Too many authors think they have something special and nobody really cares but them."

I Universe was quick to try and take the rights. They didn't like the fact that Mudflap had secured the work prior to his contact with them. The Bullies offered their contract with a large, over-sized phrase saying, "The author holds the rights." Then take the rights away with two pages of small print that only a lawyer can comprehend completely.

Jay Alden Bailey

The literary world is saturated with bullies at every level.

Many wear pouts like badges and they all think authors should be working for peanuts or free.

Mudflap, as a life-long contractor, still struggles with attitudes of the general public who at first think contractors are overpaid, then think their time is worthless and expect more and more all at no charge. That is why he bends over backward for his appreciative clients and he has no time at all for the foot stompers.

Mudflap is amazed how the literary world treats a new author and how poorly they all seem to value their time. Mudflap was even threatened by a pouting librarian.

In the State of Maine, Mudflap was glad to give away a hardcover book to the Bowerbank Library. The town was not only mentioned in the book, but they have the most inexpensive taxes absolutely possible and are truly a generous town community-wise. They are quick to help anyone in need from Mudflap's experience.

Naples, on the other hand, being in southern Maine, is a greedy town, taxing the properties to the maximum, and they are not as nice to boot. The pout is worn regularly and generosity is not what I would call an attribute Naples holds dear.

Don't ask or expect anything from Naples, they wouldn't give away ice-water in the winter.

After 35 years of residency in Naples, Mudflap knows where he stands. After his experience with librarians and the eye rollers in Connecticut, he was cautious when he approached the Naples Town Library.

Mudflap The Gloves Come Off

Mudflap had paid over $40,000 in taxes in the twenty years he owned his farm on the Burnell Road. When he purchased his Island in the town's Long Lake, the taxes were over $1,400. Then they skyrocketed to almost $5,400. Naples has billed Mudflap way over a $100,000. in the 35 years he has resided there. Add registrations and it's probably closer to $150,000.

Mudflap didn't educate his children there, have a paved road at the farm, and no road at all to the Island. (They finally paved the farm's road after he left.) He didn't get anything but grief and Flatlander talk from the inhabitants.

He approached the Library with a reluctant and skeptical attitude. The only reason he thought they would want his book was that he, the author, lived in Naples and the town was mentioned in the book.

The librarian said, "Just leave it there," and pointed at a counter. When Mudflap told her how expensive the hardcover was and he didn't want to, "just leave it", and he was hoping they would support a local author, her already sour countenance turned very bitter. She reprimanded him for even considering not giving away his book. Mudflap was ready for the attitude and replied, "Well, not only am I a 35-year resident, Naples is in the book." She replied, "Where are you from? You don't really live here." Mudflap said, "I have been pouring money into the town for three decades, educating your children and I thought you might show me a little support."

Then she really got nasty and exclaimed, "I can't support every local author who walks in with a book!" Mudflap, knowing this was going down-hill, said, "You're not the first librarian I've met with a negative attitude. You all think that books should be free and self-published authors aren't worth anything. I am not giving away my books, especially not to a greedy town like Naples. And you, along with the other librarians, are in my next book."

"You won't get anywhere if you dare criticize libraries," she said, in a threatening tone.

"Dare?" Sounds like a threat to Mudflap, sounds like censorship, sounds like a bully.

Needless to say, the two parted on a bad note.

A prior Naples Librarian experience Mudflap had ties into town politics, too. Another librarian and elected town official to the selectman's board was a Ms. Collins. (Who later advanced into a State-level position. (But not the same person as Ms. Collins the National Senator.) This high-ranking political figure in the town showed extreme unethical bias toward Mudflap because he wasn't born locally and was what they call a "Flatlander," or "Person from Away." With continuity and in step with the other librarian, Mudflap's 35-year residency and payment of the high taxes gave him no respect or courtesy at all.

Mudflap had access easement issues for rights to his Island, as the town revitalized its center. They had to restrict a free-for-all use at the town's parking and docking systems; an issue very understandable and wise, protecting the town's taxpayers.

Mudflap wanted an exception to the new rule because he had deeded rights to the Causeway for access to his island way back in the town's records.

Before his hearing at the town hall, he went to the Library to access the town's web-site records platform. The Librarian/Selectman Ms. Collins was on duty. Mudflap was having trouble with the town's site and asked Ms. Collins for assistance. She was unable to help as the town had a software upgrade issue going on and the record platform was unavailable.

At the town meeting that evening Mudflap had a simple request for overnight parking.

There at the Selectman's table was Ms. Collins and two other Selectmen. Mudflap's request came up and he was able to address the board. He explained his access needs and based his request on deeded rights he saw when researching his purchase to the Island years back, rights granted long before the town grew so very busy.

Mudflap had stayed out of town politics. He recognized all the board members from his many years of residency but didn't really know them well. One of them was a local businessman Mudflap thought would be fair. The man asked for proof of the records.

Mudflap started to explain about the records being unavailable and he was cut short, the man reprimanding him for being unprepared and wasting their time. Mudflap turned to Ms. Collins, asking for her confirmation that the town's site had problems. He was again interrupted and received another reprimand for speaking out of order. Ms. Collins acted like she didn't know what he was talking about, staying silent, even though it was that very morning that Mudflap had been at the library with her.

When Mudflap protested, the other Selectman, who had seen Mudflap around town for years, snapped at him and said, "We have heard enough."

The three board members ganged up in "bully fashion" and dismissed him on the spot, trying to humiliate him in front of the whole assembly of townsfolk.

Mudflap's decades of residency and six figures in taxes were of no value to the board of selectmen. They were mean, rude, and totally dismissive. It was a sick display of outright contempt for an out-of-state property owner. Bullies in unison, abusing their authority, and enjoying it.

Mudflap didn't want to make a federal case out of the whole thing so, to protect his investment and make it as easy for his family as possible to use their Island, he purchased a modest property in the village district for his access solution.

You know the old saying, "You can't fight city hall." Mudflap ended up forking over another $2,000 per year to do his part filling the coffers of the "Greedy Town of Naples."

In life, like war, you got to know when to retreat, regroup, and fortify.
Mudflap, Over and Out !

Arborist and Author

It's two occupations you don't usually see together.

Mudflap was called by his client:
"Rara Avis," Latin for Rare Bird.

Mudflap had been self-employed at this point for 40 years in an industry full of cutthroat businesses that open and close. Amateurs who have a chainsaw think it's fun until they get in over their heads and make a mess, or worse.

An industry that often the general public expects the professionals to compete with these amateurs, neighbors and poorly insured, (at best) poorly equipped start-up companies. Often, throughout the years, people have asked if the work could be done for no charge in exchange for the firewood.

So, Mudflap is not a stranger to the idea that people think that many occupations should work for very little or free.

He has learned along the way that many of these people are bullies who think this way, and play stupid as they feel out just how ignorant the person they have called to estimate their job really is. If they have any knowledge or experience at all they can be quite crafty in negotiating extras into a contract.

After decades of dealing with the general public, Mudflap has a leg up on being an author, an advantage most other authors don't have. There are little words that aid in the bully tactics of the public setting off alarms to seasoned professionals like, "only" and "just" for example. Those little words imply there is nothing of any real worth to the task described.

Now Mudflap, on his new business adventure of being an author, sees the similarities and is not quite as gullible as he was when starting up his tree business, or as eager to give away his efforts as he had been when young and naive.

A true self-employed person learns quickly to take opportunities seriously and act, a survival instinct of the fittest. Start-up businesses who don't act on opportunities and or procrastinate will not last.

As a start-up author, Mudflap had a huge client base he could bounce off of already established. At first, he joked that any tree service client he had who did not support his book was no longer going to get service.

All of his clients, many he considers his friends, were very supportive and pleasantly surprised that he had written a book. One lady said, "You want me to buy this book? It better be good, or you're fired." Now that's funny. That's a Mudflap-kinda joke, something he would say if the situation was reversed.

A few rolled their eyes and reluctantly bought his book, but at least they showed support so that was enough for Mudflap. Most people bought the book and haven't read it, yet. We are all busy and he understands the great majority of us struggle for reading time, if we take the time at all.

The people that actually took the time read the whole book gave very positive feedback.

There were a few people who were not only unsupportive, but had the librarian scowl, too.

One lady, after Mudflap told her how much the books cost, the trouble and time going to Washington D.C., the Library of Congress and the Patent and Trademark Office, had this to say: "What makes you think anybody would care about your idea? Why waste all the time and money?"

A gentleman Mudflap tried to sell a book to said: "Why don't you just add the cost of the book to your job and tell people you're giving it to them?"

Well, that's exactly what Mudflap wouldn't do, he never padded a job for anything.

Mudflap realized that the same people who were negative about the book, were the same people who complained about stupid stuff in their yards. They were the ones who on a regular basis were hard to deal with and generally unhappy with most everything.

So, he decided after thinking about it a while he wasn't going to work for those people anymore. There was three of them and he called each one back, being ethical and not standing them up. Mudflap is not a no-show contractor.

The first lady he fired for the scowl on her face telling her: "I don't enjoy you or your yard."

He fired the gentleman saying to him: "I would never pad a job. I only charge outright for what I think a job is worth, no more no less. And I don't want to work for somebody who would do business like that."

And the other lady gave Mudflap the most satisfying moment he ever had firing anyone, ever. He discussed the lady, her attitude and her yard with his helper. They agreed that she was nothing but trouble. So, he called her up, putting the phone on speaker, he felt they were like two little kids doing a prank call. He informed her they were not coming to work on her yard. She asked, "Are you sick? Or hurt? Why can't you make it?"

"Well," Mudflap said, "last time I was there you were mean to me and you're weird. It's a combination I just can't deal with". Before she could reply, he hung up and they rolled with laughter.

Now she has become an inside joke. They often comment when people get difficult: "You can be mean; we can deal with it. Or you can be crazy, as long as you're nice. But pick one and go, you can't be both!"

It's a Combination nobody wants to deal with.
Mudflap, Over and Out !

Librarians / Primary Residents

Book signings can be a humbling experience.

Einstein and Edison both had trouble and criticism from their teachers.

And they both lit up the world in their own special way.

Mudflap, Over and Out !

At the Authors and Publishers group Mudflap joined, one of the first things they told him was that all new books and authors are crap in a 50-mile radius of their home.

Their point being, don't let the local feedback in your area discourage you. Try to get a book signing at your local library and prepare yourself for a poor turn out.

History is littered with great people who had inspirational ideas but, at first, they were shot down. Often discredited or commonly disregarded, these people had worked hard against established narrow-minded thinking and proved to the critics that the world is not a flat place.

Education comes in many forms and the literary world is extremely important as a vehicle to push and carry knowledge forward. It's so important but many of the people in the library world forget that most "original inspirations" come from experience. And literature's job is to carry that "original idea" forward so that it can be built upon.

Most people who shoot others down never had an original idea in their heads.

Don't let anyone discourage you, especially the ones closest to you.

Mudflap, still after proving himself time and again, has to put up with the "eye rolling" and the "library scowl" of even his Sweet Little Introverted Wife, who wouldn't bully anyone.

It seems the closer to home you get, the more sharply the criticism becomes. And the more highly educated the people are, the quicker they are to disregard new or unconventional ideas.

Mudflap got a book signing scheduled at his local library. The head librarian and Mudflap's neighbor is a nice guy and showed some degree of support. He was friendly and seemed to listen to some of Mudflap's ideas. He didn't show the scowl that so many others librarians sport but there was a patronizing air about his demeanor.

Mudflap tried to brush off the negative feeling he got, trying not to be too overly sensitive but things played out proving to Mudflap that his acute awareness and ability to read people was spot on.

First of all, there was no real interest in posting Mudflap's signing event on the library site and he had to ask three times before they did anything at all. In the end they shot out something quick in an email.

By stalling and not giving the event a better post and by no follow up at all, there was no solid connection to the Town website. With not enough publicity, very few people knew about it at all.

Before the book signing, Mudflap was walking his dog one day after work. Living in the center of town, the library is on his regular route and he often spends time on the library grounds strolling and poking around after hours.

Mudflap The Gloves Come Off

The Head Librarian walks to and from work. Mudflap, who doesn't miss much, caught a glimpse of him coming from afar. The Librarian saw Mudflap and, thinking he was not in view, picked up his pace to a fast trot and skirted around the neighboring houses, cutting through the backyards to avoid Mudflap and any questions he may have about the upcoming event.

When the Saturday came, the Librarian stayed at his desk and never made a peep. Mudflap got only one person to attend the event; she had a connection to Sweet Wife through the Land Trust.

Without any support, the regular Saturday library attendees paid little or no attention to Mudflap. The 11:00 starting time came and went and Mudflap just had his one supporter to have a private chat with.

Mudflap was not surprised with the turn out, having such poor publicity. Towards the end, his help from work showed up along with his wife. (Sporting Mudflap logo baseball caps.) Mudflap was gathering up his things getting ready to leave. He noticed the Head Librarian took note of the two and their caps.

But all the silent treatment didn't bother Mudflap until another event took place.

A newcomer to town, a complete stranger, wrote his first book. He was a journalist of sorts with a degree in the field. Mudflap got an extensive write up sent to him by the library through the email.

Knowing how tough it is having a book signing in the Hooterville-type town of New Hartford, Mudflap made a point of showing up to give support to a fellow author.

His wife came, too, even though she didn't attend his own book signing. There were other attendees - as it turns out they were all related to the author. (Packing the audience!) If Mudflap hadn't come, his real attendance number would have been zero.

What bothered Mudflap was the Head Librarian's attitude. This completely unknown new person to the town had some kind of status above him. It must have been a college education, what else?

The Head Librarian ran over, all excited, and made a big introduction, going on and on. Mudflap watched him thinking, "what a jerk," he never acknowledged him or even left his desk at Mudflap's signing.

Mudflap bought a book, out of support, even though he was not impressed with the reading he did. And at a review of his book there were several instances where homophones occurred. Had Mudflap made the same mistakes in his book, the Librarians would have been rolling in the aisles.

I don't think the Head Librarian did his homework and his taste is mostly in his mouth.

If you really want to pick on him, he keeps a real crappy property, too. His place is not what Mudflap would call a great asset to the neighborhood.

It's easy to be a critic; Mudflap can roll with the best of the Literary Snobs. After a conversation with the journalist (attempting to become an author), a big issue jumped out at Mudflap. This guy used the technique of "Ghost Writing" as a Journalist. Mudflap asked, "Why not sign your work and get credit? It's not like fiction or a biography. Don't you want recognition as a Journalist?"

Mudflap was shocked at his spineless reply! He said, "I can say anything I want and don't have to put up with criticism. I can put out my views and not have to answer to the opposition."

Mudflap thinks that's on the verge of criminal, that's the kind of crap that divides America today! It does not matter if this "Journalist" has valid points, good opinions or not, he is a "Coward."

A true person for change and desire for influence puts himself out there on the line; they make their case for the issue at hand and stand proudly by that point of view.

A ghost-writing Journalist is afraid of his own content, terrified of criticism and scared that others may think he is wrong.

There's one more "Literary-World Snob" and "Neighbor" Mudflap would like to throw under the bus as he wraps up this local segment; nothing like a grade school "English Teacher" to traumatize you.

This classic old English teacher who lives down the street also has a gift shoppe in the center where she spends her off-school hours to escape the harmony and bliss of domestic life.

It's the kinda store that has nothing that anyone really needs for anything at all, a place full of knick-knacks, tacky signs and other unusable items, bird houses being the most practical thing in the entire store.

She took a few books from Mudflap on consignment, picking out one for herself to read. After a while Mudflap took the two books back that she had out on display, reason being they were getting damaged from handling and were becoming unsaleable; figuring if they were losing value and he had to give them away they might as well get into the right hands.

He didn't ask her to pay for her copy, he purposely waited until the holidays came when her cash flow would be better and she would be in a charitable holiday mood.

Jay Alden Bailey

Mean old English teachers and charitable in moods are hard to come by; statement proven when Mudflap stopped in later in December. Note first: She was the only person who didn't pay up-front for Mudflap's book.

When he stopped in as he did most every December to patronize her store and asked to be paid for the book, she was less than receptive; stating it should be free and saying something about the library. Mudflap picked up an unusable item from her shelf and asked if she would like to take the cost of the book off of the item?

Forgetting Mudflap was a store patron and a neighbor, she got very nasty and dismissive about the value of the Mudflap book itself and him as an author. In the six months she had it sitting there by her computer, she never really took the time to comprehend it with any depth at all.

It brought back memories of the cruelty his childhood English teachers displayed as they bullied little Mudflap and viciously tried pushing their will upon him.

She was in goose step with the scowling librarians, clicking her heels and demanding books should be free.

The most important thing Mudflap has learned over the time spanning his 40-year career is that everyone's time, at every level, no matter how insignificant their position may seem, has value and should be respected, period.

Maybe Librarians and the Literary Elite deep down question their own self-worth?

Makes you wonder.
Mudflap, Over and Out !

P.S. Real Time: An interesting observation: Mudflap has found out consistently that the people who skim his book, just read a segment or receive hearsay of a segment and don't spend the time to comprehend the content, all have negative attitudes and twisted opinions.

P.P.S. Real Time: Mudflap ran into the Journalist new to town on the sidewalk as he passed by Mudflap's house that was decorated in front with little boats and canoes for sale.

Mudflap recognized the man and struck up a conversation with him, slowly pulling him into debate knowing the man's extreme and narrow right-wing view of everything.

The Journalist starting talking about going south to Texas and his wonderful experience of living the right-wing dream. He was at a big ranch somewhere and was so impressed with riding around in an ATV, carrying guns, and drinking beer.

They have wild pigs tearing up the land, and ranchers have to hunt them down; he went on about how necessary guns are in managing their land.

The Journalist, obviously new to the rural way of life was so impressed with the ATVs, said, "They have these things called side by sides," as if Mudflap had never heard of them. Almost everybody has one (if they can afford it) in Bowerbank.

He went on about how important guns are to the ranchers. And how cool they were drinking beer, driving and shooting all at the same time. Then he started on about how Easterners don't understand and everyone on the east coast is a liberal.

Mudflap stopped him and pointed out that New Hartford was run by Republican Conservatives and Mudflap himself is no liberal. "So why are you here? You should move," said the Journalist.

Now Mudflap was getting offended and said, "Because I am a New Englander. I'm not going anywhere." He changed the subject and told the Journalist that he had read his book and it was filled with homophones. He tried to make a point that bad grammar hurts an author in the eyes of the literary world, reducing their credibility. He got defensive and said, "Every word in that book is there for a reason and if a homophone occurred it was on purpose." That Mudflap found humorous because he knew that there was no "pun" to the homophones; they were just plain mistakes.

Then the Journalist shifted the conversation to Mudflap's boats for sale and mentioned the antique canoe that was there. When Mudflap told him the price he indicated that he was looking for something cheaper because he was just a poor writer and needed a break.

Mudflap said, "I'm in business, and have to make money. I can't afford to give them away. I do have some less expensive ones in the back." "I'm looking to spend $50 or maybe $100", the Journalist said.

(Here we go!)
This is just what I mean about extremists, you need a pencil and paper to keep track of all their crap.
#1 Everybody in the East is not a Liberal.
#2 No real conservative would condone drinking and driving.
#3 No real "sane" conservative would drink and handle firearms, never mind drive, too.
#4 A conservative would be supportive of a small business and not expect a hand out.

#5 A conservative would have too much self-respect to whine, cry poor and ask for assistance when they really don't need it and they are just plain cheap.

#6 A real conservative would not degrade their own profession with poor sloppy work and make lame excuses for substandard quality in performance and/or workmanship.

#7 A real conservative with backbone, proud of his convictions, would not hide behind a "ghost name" when writing as a journalist.

His name is James W. Vickers, author of the homophone minefield "In Between People". I can't find any emphasis where the homophones are used to create or add anything to the book.

He doesn't come up in the journalist world in a Google search, but there are other James Vickers. He in particular is a nobody; although he is out there writing and trying to spread the two parties ever farther apart.

His rhetoric is not one of unification and forward movement. He is standing on some good right-wing policies, while discrediting the left and disregarding the moderates who want compromise.

Watch out for any of his articles and or take any journalist's work with a grain of salt if you don't recognize their name, it could be him.

Take all of his formal Journalist work as one-sided and exclusionary. He is a whiney liberal playing dress up as a tough conservative.

Mudflap thinks he should stop being a "little baby" and sign all his work like a "real man".

MF.> Out !

P.P.P.S. Real Time: To the Literary Elite --

Mudflap's first book has been put out in a second printing for the national market on Amazon. The Author spent more time refining his sentences and correcting every tiny mistake he could find. The biggest correction was more in composition as he has found his own disdain for repeating words.

The Author now understands that it's not just about a perfect grammatical sentence, it's the fact that most mistakes are plain unnecessary and show a lack of discipline, is unflattering and does to a great extent reduce the creditability of the content.

The Author now sees typos in many articles and writings of all sorts reducing his opinion of the composers. He's feeling himself becoming a bit of a Literary Snob, too.

Mudflap, Paying Tribute and Out !

Chapter 2

Local Politics

The Facilitator and the Obstructionist

One has a wide clear vision and is for progress.
(A polite, selfless, and considerate person)

The other is nearsighted, in a fog, and is narrow minded.
(A demanding, ego-based and demeaning person)

Who do you want running your town?
Mudflap, Over and Out !

(Connecticut)

New Hartford is a small town in northwestern Connecticut. Often confused with being part of Hartford, it's on the edge of Litchfield County over a half hour away. It's commutable to Hartford but not ideal. Next to Torrington (one of the biggest micropolitan cities in the entire U.S.) but not really that dependent on it. It's an old agricultural town but most people who live there are not farmers. It's in Litchfield County (New Yorker influenced) but doesn't get a lot of New York vacationers.

New Hartford is a cute and quaint little town caught in the middle of all these other places.

The real estate never booms big during good times, so it doesn't see the dramatic crashes in the recessions. It's a stable place where change comes at a turtle's pace. There is not a lot of nightlife action unless you like town committees; the town hall being the most visibly active place in the evening.

The sidewalk cafe in the center has changed hands again and the new owners frown upon the local drinking crowd. Luckily for the town, craft beer is in vogue and a brewery/pub has opened up, as well as a club in an old retrofitted factory, giving places for people who want a social/evening life to go to. There is only a handful of restaurants in town and just lately two of them closed.

The Town has assets: One of, if not the cleanest lake in the state, West Hill and the Farmington River; both have class fishing. Along with parks, protected lands and open spaces, it's a great destination place. The town tries to enhance and promote its appeal; but it's not quite there yet, it's an "undiscovered jewel." The salmon in the river attract fly-fishermen from long distances and gives the town some notoriety but little New Hartford maintains its in-between status where it seems to always find itself.

The Towns is as close to Mythical American Mayberry as you can get in New England. It's the hub of the small surrounding rural towns, carrying 70% of the regional school system's budget.

The town needs to grow but not in my back yard is the attitude. The inhabitants work hard or are retired and active with one common denominator: they like the town the way it is.

The politics are pretty clear; like many small, rural towns the conservatives are in power. They are fiscally responsible and socially conscious; thrifty is the number one policy.

When Mudflap first moved to town at only 30 years old, he was too busy working to have time to involve himself with politics.

The reality is most people are the same way; they are caught up in their daily lives, too busy working and trying to stay ahead of the bills, only catching a few minutes of a break, if that. People naively want to believe that their town officials are doing the right thing, so they go about their own business in blissful ignorance.

Being a new resident, Mudflap's first couple years in town were in social isolation, the close neighbors being the only contact he had with the local population. Mudflap learned the hard way not to flaunt his tree service at his home and didn't work for the neighbors or sell any work in town at all. He stuck to his client base in Hartford County and slipped back over the Litchfield County line to live in anonymity. He limited his exposure at the town hall to basic taxes and building permits.

It wasn't until Mudflap's wife moved in and they began having children that he got to know a lot more people. First through preschool at the church, then the schools, the library, and finally more people at the town hall.

Mudflap is known as The Tree Man of West Hartford; in New Hartford he was known to more people as Robert and Alexandra's dad.

Jay Alden Bailey

It takes three decades to become a solid member of a New England community. But just as Mudflap is still a Catholic even after a fallen status, he's still from Durham over 40 years after leaving.

Mudflap started paying attention to local politics when a new sewer plant was proposed. The town fathers/mothers pushed through the plan with over-zealous enthusiasm. Claiming to have complete transparency and aided by over-paid design engineers, they put on a show at one of the schools and pushed their agenda through.

It would take an entire book for the story but here is the fact of the matter: with limited research and no real complex study, they did not take into consideration the 100-year-old piping infrastructure and the simple math of the water volume.

They pushed a plant design through that was four times the size of the existing plant in service. Not only based on a miscalculation of water volume but of projected town growth in a historically slowly-expanding town.

This monster-size plant cost many millions despite all the grants and aid from the state. It was a staggering bill placed on the tiny user base.

The ego of the selectman in power, aided by the greed of the designers, pushed through their erroneously mathematic plan with "Bullying Hype" and speed like "Blitzkrieg". They were in a fantasy land selling a "Field of Dreams" and telling everyone, "If we build it, they will come." Oh, God, what a mistake!

The Bullies, like Nazis, pushed their vision of a perfect utopian dreamworld. And like the original Nazis, their dream came crashing down hard on them and the residential population, too.

34

Not only did they do all this projected expansion based in a historically slowly growing town, they did it right at the top of the biggest economic bubble of the new millennium.

"POP" goes the dream. And to keep in step in their Nazi style, the bullies had a serious logistics miscalculation, too. The existing water intake volume into the plant and the math of the use of each household's output on the system had a serious discrepancy that was being overlooked.

Funny how, but not in the "ha-ha" sort of way, "coincidently" the "Selectman to Be" in the future was there at the Bullies' "Nazi-style Rally" that was pushing the plan through. This common-sense guy got a moment to voice his concern about the mathematical question he had about the water usage and pointed out he saw a problem. He also was concerned about the fact that one of the biggest proponents of a new plant was the engineering contractor who was obviously going to highly profit from the approval of the plan.

But the hype of the rally and the Bullies' loud voices shouting out their propaganda drowned out the "Sensible Voice of Reason." In the end, the oversized plant was passed and built.

Next came the reality of the bill. The Main Street and Downtown user base got handed one of the highest monthly sewer rates in the state, followed by the big recession.

The dream of the expanding town's population that was supposed to help pay for the loan did not happen, leaving a small group with a stupid, over-sized plant and bill.

The reality of the town's over-zealous and outright bad leadership decisions made by the town's "Fuhrer," led to the fall of his administration.

The man we will call "The Sensible Voice of Reason" eventually took over and with his "Allies" they got stuck cleaning up the mess.

Having to address the skyrocketing cost of maintaining a bigger plant with bigger maintenance issues, they also had to address the piping infrastructure problems. In the process a discovery was made. A leak in the pipes wasn't letting water out, it was taking water in. The plant was processing clean ground water at an incredible rate. The leak was addressed and the consumption of water was dramatically reduced. The water volume had been miscalculated with the voodoo math of the Bully Builders who had pushed the oversized, over-exaggerated, and unnecessarily large plant.

To add insult to injury, the tiny user base was forced to pay a staggering bill for the construction of this giant mistake they didn't make. Like many downtowns, a high percentage of the people on the system were the most financially strapped part of the population. The properties affected were condos, an affordable housing project, two-family houses, apartment buildings and the downtown houses with big tax bills and fallen values.

The Bullies who forced the blundered plan on the population had their higher-value properties off the system and shrugged off the problem, laying it on the backs of the people in town who could afford it the least. What a classic act!

The new administration was left with an understandably aggravated group of disgruntled people, receiving criticism and years of aggravation. The issue dropped real estate values and impeded economic growth for many years that followed.

The outcome of the Bullies' influence took a slowly expanding town's turtle pace and reduced it to an inch worm's progress. The only real estate seeing any noticeable increase in value were the more high-end homes. A snap-shot of America, where the wealthy grow fatter and the poor struggle to survive.

Start paying attention, you could find yourself helping your town and be a "Sensible Voice of Reason."
Mudflap, Over and Out !

Vacationland

Disconnecting and Unplugging is a Good Thing.

Go Acoustic !
Mudflap, Over and Out !

(Maine)

Being exposed to a different world in the State of Maine, Mudflap saw there too, a struggle of the poor working class and the wealth of the multi-homes class. The wealthy flaunt their excess and build oversized and completely unnecessary opulent homes; taking cute small cottages on the sea shore and lakes and over-build them. In the process they increased the values, which increased the taxes and made it impossible for most local people to afford the waterfront in their own home towns.

There is a form of bullying that comes naturally when wealth interacts with the impoverished. People who come to these communities with more resources than the local population can play "The Big Fish in a Little Pond" game.

Mudflap himself had used the advantage of taking the resources from Connecticut and using those resources in the more financially challenged regions of Maine.

After many years of having property in Maine, Mudflap saw a phenomenon typical in vacation-oriented communities; he now sees this phenomenon playing out in his primary home town, too.

People from away, as they are called, (especially retired people) buy property in vacation-oriented places. At first, they are captivated by the contrast of life in the different place that they have chosen to live in part time.

The whole reason they chose to have a vacation home in the first place is the contrast in the way of life the other place has to offer; as well as the geographical differences, as in the features like, oceans, lakes, mountains, woods, deserts and so on.

Once settled in and enjoying their new-found environment, these people from away (many who are retired) with too much time on their hands get involved in the town's politics.

(Here we go!) First these people start graciously, giving their time volunteering to sit on boards they have interests in. Depending on their primary home status, (many happen to choose the vacation community for tax purposes), they may even get a seat on the board of selectmen.

Then they start to criticize the way things are run and they want the town to be more like where they came from. As their influence grows, they become more and more righteous; then their mission changes from a charitable gift of their time to saving the town from itself.

The locals have become aware of such people and it doesn't help nurture a positive attitude.

Back some time ago, way up country in Mudflap's most northern outpost of Bowerbank, Maine, such a phenomenon played out in its entirety.

Bowerbank has absolutely no town ordinances at all, period. The only ordinances they abide by is what the State requires. That's it, nothing else; the residents feel that you should be able to do what you want with your own property. Many are self-employed, running business out of their residence. There is no such thing in the town as commercial property; all the land is useable for whatever the owner wants it to be used for. This is small town government not telling you to do anything extra than the state laws dictate.

A true conservative community; unlike the national conservative right who are becoming more and more increasingly invasive, trying to micro manage our everyday lives.

The National Republican Party has ceased to be conservative and is more a form of communism, except without the social benefits. And now it even has a fascist tone to it where a president can go rogue and no longer has to answer to anyone for his actions.

Add cameras on your TVs and computers, microphones and GPS on our phones, and Big Brother in Orwell's *1984* is here. Include throw-away product technologies, legalized marijuana (like Soma keeping the masses complacent) and Huxley's Brave New World is here, too.

Science fiction keeps becoming real; yeah, it's becoming really scary.

Back to Bowerbank, a land of true conservatives. When Mudflap and the "Infamous Lady with Six Kids" first bought Phoebe Island, their view up the lake was bare shoreline with a few camp houses to their side. A decade later the lots on shore went up to $25,000 and then shot to $90,000 and now these days they have pretty much become unavailable.

Of course, they didn't build seasonal camp cottages; they are full-sized, year-round homes. Sebec is an up-country lake with many residents from Maine; but the "People from Away" or Flatlander's have infiltrated the community and the local politics, too.

After they got their homes the way they wanted them, using the limited restrictions required in Bowerbank (Like putting a garage right next to the property line, etc.) they decided that no future home owner should have the same liberties that they enjoyed.

So, these retired guys from away with too much time on their hands got it in their heads that Bowerbank needed saving from itself. And saving from neighbors like them that do what they want with their buildings and put monster size houses on undersized lots, etc., etc., etc.

The retired schmucks who were playing politicians, put together the first comprehensive zoning plan ever proposed in Bowerbank. There were pages of complex restrictions and laws all designed to reign in the behavior of the wild-west style townspeople.

The locals are all hard-working regular people, who were too busy trying to make ends meet to pay attention to what their neighbors were doing. On top of it, they have too much respect for their neighbors to care.

The retirees, having all the time in the world, tried to slip the laws through while the local population was busy working.

Well, they thought they were smarter than the locals. They thought the locals were ignorant because they didn't have as much money. Just because they mind their own business doesn't mean they are not paying attention.

There is a high percent of people from away who own property and wanted the zoning passed. But not being primary residents, they get no vote, only the few full-time retirees could vote.

An extensive package of the proposed laws was handed out to all homeowners.

Mudflap couldn't believe all the new laws and how many people were actually for it, the whole thing was turning into a battle.

As Mudflap read the laws, some things jumped out at him he didn't like and he thought time was running out and he had better act and do some things to get grandfathered in on some of the laws.

One dumb thing they listed was: No fence posts could be placed on the ground. They all had to be dug in. What crazy person would not dig in their fence post? Maybe somebody like Mudflap.

Well, the ground in parts of Bowerbank is extremely rocky, "boney" is the term.

Mudflap wanted some posts by his land's multiple entrances; he didn't want to spend his summer with a pick axe so he placed posts in buckets and filled them with cement.

Next law he didn't like was against signs, so up went the signage he wanted.

And, the last and the most important law he didn't like was the law against shipping containers.

Flatlanders and People from Away DON'T LIKE CONTAINERS !

Mudflap had one brought in ASAP and that completed all his sinful hick-type property amenities. (We won't call them improvements.)

Mudflap, ahead of the curve, relaxed and conceded to the fact that times were changing and so was Bowerbank.

Not so fast, Flatlanders !

The locals rallied (all 96 of them) and people who usually are too busy to bother came to the defense of true conservatism.

They shot down the retired know-it-all "Bullies"! Put them in their place and threw away all the many hours and months of tedious work and research that was done to save these poor, ignorant, backwoods people from the horrors of true independence.

To this day Bowerbank only abides by what the State of Maine requires, period.

Larger towns across America should take a tip from little Bowerbank and review their local laws.They may find some outdated, unnecessary and some may be too restrictive, stifling economic growth. Many of these laws may infringe on the true conservative way and impede the path of the liberals, too.

It never hurts to review and update.
Mudflap, Over and Out !

Jay Alden Bailey

Facilitating

When the ball's in the air it's anybody's game.

Grab it and run !
Mudflap, Over and Out !

Mudflap likes history and we should take notes and remember lessons. Many times, it's one person who comes up, often unassuming or not necessarily at the top of command, but they come to the plate and change the course of battles, wars and history itself.

A couple of Mudflap's favorites are:

#1 Richard Winters, D-Day Paratrooper, who fought through to the end of the Second World War in Europe.

All his superiors were killed on the landing. He rallied his men and won the objective on the first day. He took the opportunity given to him and ran with it. The kinda person who changes history and is a facilitator who gets things done.

#2 Armstrong Custer, best remembered for being slaughtered at the Little Big Horn, did actually do a great thing to save the Union in the Civil War.

At Pickett's Charge in Gettysburg, the South had their cavalry coming up from behind to split the Union forces in a simultaneous action, as Pickett's men did their frontal assault on Cemetery Ridge. This climatic battle of the war was won with the help of Custer; as he found the South's cavalry coming through a narrow pass and hit the front of their line with his smaller cavalry.

Another small Union cavalry saw what Custer was doing and came to assist; together they stopped the advance of the South. Since the South's cavalry never made it to assist Pickett, the charge failed, and the course of the battle, the war and history itself was changed.

So, Custer was a hero; too bad it went to his head and he thought himself invincible. With no war to feed his ego, he turned his focus to the genocide of the Native Americans. The immoral quest and his disrespect of humanity left him the unflattering legacy he enjoys today.

A good lesson for those who never seem to have enough of anything like, glory, money, fame, luxury, power and so on. Often you got to know when to be happy and just plain give it a break.

Sometimes someone who appears to facilitate may be an obstructionist in disguise; bringing disaster with his poor and or over-zealous actions. Often the common denominator you can use to see the difference is whether that person is acting in the best interests of everyone, or only a certain group or special interest. Hail Hitler, history's most famous Bully; facilitator in disguise. The most totally warped obstructionist of modern times. He could have been the world's most accomplished statesman but with his focus so narrow he excluded way too many people and failed.

We could go further and blame the French for the Second World War, since they were the Bullies during the Treaty of Versailles. They were "thugs" like crime bosses, being unreasonable only because they had muscle behind them in the form of the United States who unfairly turned the tables on the Germans by getting involved in the European war. Sticking our noses in helped set the stage for Hitler's rise.

Don't we ever learn? The United States had to oppose Russia when they were cleaning out the terrorists in Afghanistan. They actually had it right and they could be the ones still there, but no we wanted to trade places.

Sticking our noses in helped set the stage for bin Laden's rise.

Do you like the way Korea worked out?

We forgot Vietnam pretty fast and the soldiers who fought for us, too.

See any continuity?

Are we happy now?

We need real Facilitators not narrow-minded Obstructionists.

We need Moderates in power who care about the country as a whole, not just one-sided leaders.

Remember James Baker who served in Washington through multiple administrations? Interesting how one person could last through so many different leaders with all sorts of conflicting issues and policies; and being able to negotiate the changing times as well.

Change always has to start at home, then pushed out into the world. Back to local politics.

New Hartford has a person like Baker, with wide, clear vision so pristine we will call her Crystal. She has expertise comprised from years of practical experience servicing the town through multiple administrations. Crystal is not a Democrat or Republican, she's not extreme in one way or another. Or on any side other than the right one and that's what's right for everybody.

46

When asked a question you can count on a straight answer; crystal clear with nothing vague. If she doesn't know the answer to a question she will say, "I'll get back to you," and will follow it up without a second request, all in a polite and totally professional manner.

And working regular hours is a joke; Crystal stays all the time very late for all sorts of meetings and activities, helping to facilitate progress for different boards. She is called upon for protocol answers in many diverse formats.

I have seen a whole large room of people wait in practically breathless silence for her to return with paperwork or an answer to a protocol question. Talk about a facilitator, the town hall almost can't move without her. The town owes her more than they will ever pay her. No matter what, we are indebted to her.

To Crystal it's not about the money, it's about getting things right.

She is also at town social events and projects, like kids painting town-approved graffiti on the center's sidewalks and other fun events.

Not only does Crystal not lean right or left politically, but when it comes to budget or town service issues, any influence she may have, (and she has lots of influence) personally she has not one ulterior motive whatsoever. She does not live in New Hartford.

Crystal is the most completely fair, un-biased, neutral, and totally dedicated to her job and community person that Mudflap has ever encountered in his life.

It never ceases to amaze him how often she continues to prove these facts over and over again.

Mudflap is going somewhere with this: "Obstructing!"
Over and Out !

Obstructing

Often Bullies have grandiose ideas and lofty goals.

Keep it moderate.

Keep it real.
Mudflap, Over and Out !

The town of New Hartford has three selectmen; the first selectman is a paid job and it's the number one position. The second selectman (a volunteer) is the running mate of the first selectman. The third (volunteer) is selectman by default for the opposite party who loses the race. In this case the selectman by default is a Democrat.

The rest of all the town's Commissions and Boards from finance to zoning, recreation to open space, 32 in all, are positions run by volunteers; that is a lot of dedicated people.

Speaking of dedicated people, the second selectman, the "Numbers Lady," has tirelessly dedicated herself for many years at no cost to the town. A professional auditor by trade she literally watches every dollar spent by the town and cares about every expenditure as if it were her own grandmother's last dime. A remarkably loyal and uncommon selfless community member.

One evening Mudflap attended a selectmen's meeting where they were approving a conservation easement his Sweet Wife was working on with her cohort in effort, both women of the Land Trust.

Another approval being put through was a new park: Land to be leased at one dollar a year for 25 years, with an option for 25 more, by a family who had already been so philanthropic to the town that a library was named after them. There is a good chance after 50

49

years the land would go to the town permanently. Regardless, it was a nice thing for the town to be able to expand its recreational destination appeal that it's trying to move towards; the gift pushing to aide future economic development plans.

As the selectmen went to approve the new park, a gentleman stood up in defiance of the approval. Mudflap thought he was strange because it sounded like a good thing for the town's residents, as well as increasing the destination appeal. But this man wanted the park approval put on stall and demanded a committee be formed to review the idea. The selectman said, "Stalling approval would send a bad message to the philanthropic family. No, we are moving to approve."

The man interrupted again and quoted some protocol rule. The First Selectman looked towards Crystal and she gave her statement on topic and rule of meeting.

(Here we go!) The man out of order loudly exclaimed, "Why are we listening to her? She's just some town employee."

There was a moment of silence, Mudflap not believing his ears. Did this guy know who he was talking about? He received a reprimand from the Chair and he sat down with a pout and one last out-of-order remark.

Mudflap was offended, what a jerk; he should be taken out into the hall and flogged on the spot!

This man really rubbed Mudflap the wrong way and it continued to bother him so he started asking questions like, "Who is that guy?" The answer: "Mr. Rosengrim, the new Democratic selectman who won by default. This is the last meeting of his predecessor. He will be sitting at the table next month."

"Really?" thought Mudflap. (The switch flipped.) This guy is a bad apple, a problem for the board and a problem for the town. This particular meeting was in the big hall upstairs for larger groups during bigger agenda meetings. Mostly the selectmen meetings are unattended by the public and are held in the small conference room on the first floor.

Next selectmen meeting, Mudflap attended. Prior to the meeting Mudflap had visited Crystal in her office and apologized for not speaking up in her defense at the last large agenda. They had a nice conversation and he got a lock on Rosengrim's attitude and demeanor.

The first Selectman who knows Mudflap was surprised to see him attending as did his partner. Crystal hadn't given Mudflap's intention away; he was there to see how Rosengrim was going to behave at his first formal meeting sitting at the selectmen's table. (Public seating is around the side walls and they are not allowed a voice until the end at public comment time.)

Note: Mudflap gets a kick out of attending meetings after work before he cleans up. He smiles to himself as he looks at everybody all spiffy in their cute shoes and nice shirts while Mudflap is in dirty, ripped, permanently stained clothes and work boots to match. In the warm weather he's dressed again in dirty rags: ripped up tank top and shorts with boots, sporting a hard tan and always a layer of saw dust topping off any and all outfits.

Mudflap feels he is the voice of the common working man who is too tired from a long day and wants to be with his family in the evenings. Too bad for the Bullies, now Mudflap's kids are grown up; he can give his Sweet Wife a break, too, and be on somebody else's case.

They started out all peaceful-like, trying to get through the agenda, but Rosengrim didn't take long to attack. New Hartford needs to move and improve the town garage. They have a plan and have spent money to stall the move, holding out for the best financial outcome possible.

This is a thrifty board, pinching pennies, repairing police cars and town trucks, rather than purchasing new equipment. Mudflap attended meetings years back and stopped going because he saw no need to look over their shoulders, they are outright cheap and squeeze every dime; remember the right-hand selectman #2 is "The Numbers Lady."

This new selectman had all sorts of things he disagreed with right off the bat. At the first meeting he had a list of complaints and insults of incompetence. "You dropped the ball," he said on one issue and every item he made into a case. To top it off, he is a lawyer and another "Retiree Bully" too, saving the town from itself.

To complete the phenomena, he's a transplant (a person from away), originally a Hartford-area professional. He comes in and buys one of the most expensive houses in town, then starts getting on boards and throwing his weight around. Now he is a selectman by default, didn't really get a lot of votes; only reason he's on the board is nobody on the Democratic committee wanted the position.

He made a big mistake insulting Crystal at the large meeting; Mudflap was all over him like a cheap suit when public comment time came.

Rosengrim couldn't understand why the selectmen were paying outright for things. He saw no problem bullying them with talk of debt. He said, "Everybody is in debt," and they were fools paying cash for things. He couldn't understand that not only were they saving interest, but debt would burden future budgets not even passed yet. He bullied and accused them of incompetence, and he wanted to pay professionals to do studies for equipment issues, building sites, and engineering plans for his proposed ideas.

The selectmen were talking about the repair of an extremely expensive roadside bush hog mower. Rosengrim wanted to hire a third party for an evaluation, not trusting the estimate to the mechanic.

He bitched and moaned on almost every line item. He's a lawyer and everything is an argument, everyone is on trial. And he knows everybody's job better than they do. He was aggressive, disrespectful, condescending, and plain bully rude.

A rich lawyer with a million-dollar house who wants debt and a new garage, "right now," stop putting it off. He talked about how nice the neighboring town's new garage was. Yah, that's because New Hartford pays for 70% of the regional school's budget for that neighboring town's kids.

He wanted a new community center built for the town and wanted it to include an upgrade for the senior center, too.

At the first meeting, he wanted to spend millions and debt the tax payers. This is the kinda guy who gives the Democrats a bad name.

Simultaneously, the selectmen were in the middle of trying to fix the town's biggest problem. They were negotiating a sale of the oversized sewer plant, that the town had been burdened with for years from the last Democrat who saw no problem with extensive debt. The WPCA (Water Pollution Control Authority) had become insolvent. After years of struggle, the issue had come to a head and the WPCA was imploding.

Coincidentally, Rosengrim was on a committee who helped push the overbuilt, understudied plant debacle. A smaller assistant bully at that point, now he felt it was his time to rise and to challenge the "Sensible Voice of Reason."

Jay Alden Bailey

Mudflap had done a little homework and found out through social channels Rosengrim's mission: this rising bully has his eyes set on the top spot, wanting to knock down the Sensible Voice, re-claim power for the Reich and become the re-established Town Fuhrer.

Mudflap had a mission of his own: to challenge the Bully Rosengrim, disrupt, distract, and discredit him at every level, at any and all venues, meetings, and social settings. He even went as far as to change parties from Republican to a Democrat to challenge him within his own party.

(Here we go!) Mudflap was loading for bear and going in for the kill relentlessly.

Mudflap picked him apart and shot down all he could in the short time the he was given a voice on the floor.

Toward the end of the meeting Rosengrim asked Mudflap, "Who are you?" Mudflap introduced himself. He then asked the question again, "Who are you?" For some reason Mudflap's name was not enough, he needed a title, so Mudflap replied, "A resident, I live here, got any problem with that?"

His eyes widened and sheepishly he said, "No."

As the meeting adjourned, Mudflap had another question. A common practice at meetings, but it would not make it into the formal minutes. Rosengrim was completely dismissive, would not talk to Mudflap, and walked away.

"Oh, is this how we are going to play?" thought Mudflap. He wants to be a bully then run away? Old Mudflap has been in bully games with tougher guys than this twerp, he thought to himself.

He cornered Rosenegrim and asked him another question. When he tried to step away without a reply, Mudflap stepped in his way, separating him from the group leaving the room, and quietly said to him so only he could hear, "You got no balls, how dare you walk away when I am talking to you."

Rosengrim got flustered, he was clearly not used to someone standing up to him as defiant as Mudflap. Crystal had told Mudflap his tactic was to attack people like adversaries and wear them down. Well, he had met his match this time; like a big old snapping turtle, Mudflap locks his jaw and down into the muck he will pull you.

Mudflap started attending every board meeting he could from finance, to open space, until the next selectmen's meeting came. He was gathering data and preparing for his next go around with Rosengrim.

At his second meeting, even though the questions were answered about all his grandiose projects, studies and law consulting, etc., etc., Rosengrim was back, talking about many of the same things with the same aggressive demeanor. Mudflap noticed that Selectman #2's usual calm, polite attitude was now defensive and edgy. She clearly was not comfortable and the apprehension showed when dealing with Rosengrim.

A special meeting was called for the proposed sewer plant sale: The solution was to privatize the sewer plant and relieve the overwhelming burden the town had been faced with for the many years that followed the debacle.

Even the usually emotionally level and professional demeanor of Crystal was being tested as "Grim" demanded more documents be available at his and everyone's fingertips for review and scrutiny. He acted as if "The Sensible Voice of Reason" had created the mess to begin with. Forgetting or denying the fact that he had taken part in allowing the stupid thing to be built in the first place.

The third Selectmen meeting was on the proposed new budget for the upcoming fiscal year:

Unbelievably, Grim was like a broken record with a skipping annoyance. Eyes rolled and Mudflap got a few smiles from Selectman #2 and Crystal, his presence now giving some relief to these dedicated ladies who were showing appreciation for his support. It wasn't really funny but you had to laugh to yourself as it was so obvious Grim was struggling, even stuttering a little as he grasped for things to complain about.

He even stated that taxes should be raised as they hadn't been for 10 years. That fact was completely erroneous; Mudflap was aware that there has been increases. Grim probably didn't notice because five or six hundred bucks doesn't mean much to him.

It's not how much you make, it's what you spend proportionally; it takes a lot of work to have five hundred dollars at the end of a month "after" all your expenses.

Grim was completely detached from the struggle of the common person. His focus was to bully the board and try to get to some kind of status level only he and his twisted ego could see.

All the board could do was grit their teeth, bite their tongues, and maintain a professional posture; their job was to stay focused on the practical realities of the chores ahead of them.

Grim's obstructionist behavior was anti-productive, slowed down progress, and was just a plain drag.

Mudflap fights on. Over and Out !

Small Town Political Postures

Stability / Integrity
They go hand in hand.

Pub Politics
Is fist to fist

Click Politics
That's "Mean Girl Style."

Mudflap, Over and Out !

(Cow Town, Durham, Connecticut)
(Old Industry, Portland, Connecticut)
(Vacationland, Naples, Maine)

The first three small towns Mudflap lived in all had different types of political formats; he didn't get involved personally but was aware and observed.

When Mudflap grew up in Durham, everybody, even the kids knew the town selectman Charlie Wimler. He ran unopposed for at least 25 years and was clearly the most respected person in the community. Nobody would think he would do anything that wasn't in the best interest of the town. His construction company did all the road plowing and maintenance, a practice that would be considered unethical, a conflict of interest, and outright criminal in today's world.

Mudflap would be shocked if he were to learn that Charlie took one dollar more than he deserved or that he did anything unethical at all. It was a time of trust and confidence in local government that is lost today.

Charlie finally retired and his company eventually stopped doing all the work around town to the great dismay of all who lived there; truly the end of an era.

I have no doubt someone had some criticism somewhere, it's the way of the world. But what passed was an innocence so pure we didn't even know we had it till we look back through time.

Mudflap has a limited opinion on Portland, Connecticut politics where he first owned property in the late '70s though the mid-'80s. At that time there were 11 places that served or sold alcohol in the small-sized town. (Not including grocery stores.)

The Portland politics were most clearly defined as follows: A bar for the Firemen, a bar for the Bikers, a bar for the Irish, a bar for the Italians, a bar for the Hippies, and a restaurant for a group like the John Birch Society (A Northern version type of KKK), later it turned into a Cowboy bar.

It was politically incorrect and outright dangerous to cross lines into any of these social circles.

Naples, Maine, where Mudflap has been a part time resident since 1985, has a political clique system where very few are ever really accepted as part of the town. Many residents are considered more like inventory than citizens: a New England mentality of precedence, combined with a frustration that they really are more like Flatlanders than Mainers.

Naples is kinda caught in the middle and undecided about a lot of things. Mudflap has been there longer than any of the town office employees, even the most senior town clerk; she is great and is an old friend. But Mudflap can't help himself reminding her every once and a while that he knew Jenny and Anne, the two old girls who ran the town's office for the century prior to Judy's reign.

Local politics is something you should at least pay attention to and, if you can, do something even if it's small. Everyone giving a little for the better of the rest, that's community, that's progress.

Keep your eyes open.
Mudflap, Over and Out !

Jay Alden Bailey

Obstructing the Obstructionists

Fight Fire with Fire.

Dig a few Trenches, too !
Mudflap, Over and Out !

(New Hartford, Connecticut)

Mudflap, now attending town meetings of all sorts, was sitting in on Economic Development. At first, he questioned them about a key property that the town needed developing, but was on stall due to the economy and the slow pace of New Hartford's growth. Mudflap thinks the town should keep petitioning the owner and incentivize him.

He went to a second Economic Development meeting and had some other ideas to run by them. As an observer or resident, you must stay quiet and you get only a limited time to make any comments or suggestions.

These board members don't seem to like resident observers, preferring to operate in a vacuum. They have little faces on, stern countenances, and, when questioned or when suggestions are made, those stern faces quickly turn to pouts. They are very defensive; how dare you have any ideas to run by them.

Mudflap had a little list that grew as the meeting progressed. As the items piled up, he started trying to prioritize them, knowing he had to make points with focus and quickly, too.

There was a lull in the meeting and the Chair asked, "Is there any other business up for discussion?" Mudflap raised his hand and the Chair asked, "What do *you* want?" Mudflap replied, "I have some economic development ideas." The Chair stated, "We don't

60

have time, we have to do the budget. So, Mudflap waited through the budget review.

They supported a Farm Day, which was a good thing and Mudflap understood the need to promote events like Bunny Day and The Tree Lighting, etc., but he was in awe that most of the time was spent talking about Easter eggs and flashlights on key rings. There was time spent on the unavailability of inexpensive senior and/or start-up homes; but it was more of a venting and a show of frustration, with no ideas or ability to resolve the issue.

As the flashlight cost and expenditure topic went on and on, Mudflap was becoming disillusioned. Finally, when it seemed they couldn't stretch out the discussion any longer, the Chair turned to him and asked, "So what did you want?" and offered up her hand in a gesture for Mudflap to speak.

Mudflap got up from his outer seat and took the guest spot at the end of the conference table to be in view of all the stern faces. Knowing he had to be quick, his first comment and recommendation was that the board should be better connected to the other boards in town.

Mudflap explained that he was sitting in on different boards and realized by listening in that they miss things and didn't really know what the others were thinking and or doing.

He suggested that each member pick a board to sit in on (Selectmen, Finance, Recreation, etc.) as liaisons and report back to the Economic Development Committee. They were all quiet, sullen; Mudflap went on. He suggested working with zoning to ease or drop restrictions, opening up opportunities for expanded use of properties. He suggested Main Street should be more commercialized for offices and shops etc.

Then he was stopped and they started shooting at him.

First, a lady interrupted and said, "We have no control over zoning, there are State Statutes," not understanding that town zoning laws could be changed. He gave his Maine town of Bowerbank as an example and she quickly shot him down saying, "That's Maine, not here."

A gentleman said, "You can already have offices on Main Street," not understanding Mudflap wanted the scope opened up even more.

The Chair said, "We can read the minutes of other boards," not recognizing that everything doesn't make the minutes and without representation they have no ability to interact.

Mudflap went on to mention the same property he pointed out at the first meeting could be used for the senior and start up level homes they wanted; and could also offer higher end units, too, with river views, making it more appealing for contractors to build.

The lady who shot down his zoning idea, jumped down his throat and said, "You already brought up that property before." Mudflap tried to explain that it tied in with what they were discussing that evening.

Mudflap started to get defensive, knowing they were about to cut him off. He mentioned their focus on eggs and Bunny Day saying, "There are bigger issues." He fit in some of Grim's bad advice and was trying to bring up incentive ideas when the Chair stopped him and called the meeting to adjourn.

They obviously did not want any of his ideas or advice. The most senior aged lady of the group did thank him for taking an interest in the town in a sincere fashion.

Mudflap The Gloves Come Off

Mudflap went to the zoning office the next day and spent two hours discussing restrictions for business and residential properties; the scope of town, neighborhood view points, and the combined effect on decisions made for each property as an individual issue.

He found out that no broad law could be passed, dropped or amended to blanket an area. The officer pointed out that variances and adjusted leniency were done on a case by case basis. He gave Mudflap a thick book of local town zoning laws for review and reference.

The Voice of Reason happened to stop into the office during the visit and agreed with Mudflap that zoning and economic development did go hand in hand. He took some time to explain more perspectives on the bigger picture of things.

Now Mudflap had more facts to bring back before the pouting faces.

On his way out he stumbled into one of the town's more influential and dedicated facilitators.

Coincidentally, the conversation circled around the many facts causing obstruction in town progress and back around to Grim, expanding Mudflap's view of the scope of the situation.

Down the rabbit hole and into a bucket of smelly worms so deep that the bottom has long ago rotted through and is long gone.

The layers of hypocrisy are so thick they have solidified around Grim until he has no spiritual movement at all; his actions had become entirely ego based with complete "Argumentative Bully Force".

Mudflap felt himself falling into a dark place, realizing his initial reaction and gut feeling about Grim was only the tip of a long bloody sword.

Mudflap was becoming overwhelmed by the negative forces he was encountering. He felt himself being knocked back, realizing that the Bully tactics of Grim and the Pouting Faces were focused on the demoralization of any who dare speak their minds and try to stand up to them.

All that the Bullies know how to do is obstruct, stonewall ideas, and grind down their opponents.

First Grim had set off the alarms on Mudflap's radar.

Reacting to the alarms, Mudflap looked for Allies. Stumbling into Economic Development he found it was lost in a quagmire of poor leadership, accented by limited ideas and negative attitudes.

They were like fish caught in shallow water, flopping around, with no ability to swim and not understanding where they were or how to get out into the deeper pool.

He looked for stability in the most important board of all, Finance. On the surface it looked solid, most all members conservative and cautious with stern sober faces, all sitting around debating the issues.

A couple of these level-headed conservatives had obstructionist agendas of their own too. Like the fallen "Liberal Reich" that over built the sewer plant, they had their view with personal motives that excluded others. (Here we go!) There were two that jumped out into Mudflap's radar.

The first one Mudflap remembered from the local bank. When he first moved into town as a new resident and businessman, he looked for a banking connection close to home. He was shot down quickly for a simple loan on a simple project that he was using purposely as a test of sorts, feeling out the demeanor of the local bank.

Years later an elementary school was closing across the other side of town because of a low attendance issue and for financial consolidation.

The Bakersville section wanted to keep its quaint and convenient school setting, better for their particular village but financially bad for the town as a whole. Mudflap understood the desire of the village and the nostalgia they were trying to keep at the expense of the rest of the uninvolved town. It was put to a vote in a referendum. Mudflap has good exposure for political signage on Main Street so he posted support for the school and for Bakersville.

At a Republican picnic, Mudflap was approached by the Banker from the old days of his first town interaction. He was complemented for showing support from across town, disregarding his own finances for the better lifestyle of Bakersville. (Not a necessity.)

He thanked the Banker and said, "It's all about community and I hope you show support likewise for the Town Center and help relieve the burden placed on the Downtown Community by the sewer plant debacle." (A necessary utility.)

The Banker took an instant 180 degree turn and said, "Why should I support the sewer plant when I get no help for my septic system?"

"Because it's town infrastructure," said Mudflap. "like a bridge or school. And it was also a catastrophic blunder made by the leaders of the town, not the poor user base who are stuck with the bill. They should pay for processing the water and running the plant but not the mistake of overbuilding the system."

The Banker walked away in a snit spoiling the feel-good moment of the original compliment.

Now that the WPCA (The Water Pollution Control Authority) had become insolvent, the user base was being over-charged and the whole system was collapsing. The Voice of Reason and his Allies had been mopping up the mess caused by the former Bullies of the past administration for years.

Luckily for the town, a professional water company was agreeing to purchase the system; the Allies had worked hard to make a good deal with thousands of hours of work and documents with complete transparency, holding everyone's hands, and going through years of meetings.

It was now before the Board of Finance for final approval. Mudflap couldn't understand why this one particular board member kept protesting redundantly; so, he did some research and found out something interesting.

The second obstructionist didn't want to see the system purchased out of fear of a personal assessment (potentially) in the far future because her house was on the outskirts of the final reach proposed on the map submitted. Her property was so far off at the edge that most likely she would be dead before the system ever expanded that far.

But fear of the water corporation who was buying the system, fear of losing control, and fear of paying more out of her own pocket to help the town as a whole was causing this volunteer board member to obstruct and potentially stop the sewer plant sale.

Aiding in the obstruction was Good Old Grim making demands of his own, acting like the Voice of Reason and the Allies were doing something wrong. Acting as if he was <u>not</u> one of the original Bullies who had pushed the whole giant mistake on the town to begin with.

Bully Grim, in complete denial, was playing Bully again, the only roll he knows.

Mudflap was sickened by Grim; he was repulsed by the Bully leading the board, aided by the underling pest with the pouting face. He was starting to feel negative himself, the forces of the dark side pulling at him. Mudflap could feel the bad energy sliding up into his spine as he started to wish he had stayed home, ignored the town hall, and just lived in blissful ignorance.

He wanted to be selfish and go out and just have fun, stay in to watch a show, anything but be near the negative energy.

Mudflap was reminded of what's important, he channels history; he remembered a story he had heard.

WWII Germany: Pastor Martin Niemoller (1892-1984):

**First, they came for the socialists, and I did not speak out—
Because I was not a socialist.
Then they came for the trade unionists, and I did not speak out—
Because I was not a trade unionist.
Then they came for the Jews, and I did not speak out—
Because I was not a Jew.
Then they came for me—and there was no one left to speak for me.**

So, disillusioned and tired of the bad energy, he channeled his British side; he put his chin up and went to the next meeting.

The Parks and Recreation Committee saved Mudflap with a bright light that shown through the darkness. They all smiled and were glad he attended. They let him sit at the table, enter the discussions and were all upbeat and positive. (It must be the exercise and clean air they get.)

They recharged Mudflap's worn-down batteries, gave him a better attitude and a shield of sorts against the pouting faces.

Mudflap fought on.

A snapshot of small-town America and local politics.

If you want things to be better, pull your head out of wherever it's stuck and get involved.

If you want to be safe and live in blissful ignorance, enjoy it, but don't complain if things don't go your way.

Mudflap, Over and Out !

P.S. Real Time: This local story with Grim was the most current of all in the book, in Real Time already.

I was trying to put the chapter to rest and move on but Mudflap didn't realize just how much trouble he was getting himself into.

{{{SIMULTANEOUSLY THE CORONA VIRUS HIT AMERICA}}} Hold on to your toilet paper!

Mudflap had gone to Zoning to ask questions for the Economic Development Board. After he left the Zoning Office, The New Young Officer, just hired in the last year, decided to investigate Mudflap and his properties in New Hartford.

Like the Bowerbank crowd and local ordinances, every town has their laws and views.

The young ambitious Zoning Officer first called the health department and made a complaint about Mudflap's house on Main Street.

Way back, when Mudflap first moved into New Hartford, he took his two-family house and renovated it with what was left of his original bridge loan money, after the Blood Sucking Divorce Lawyers took their cuts.

He put in three more bathrooms and turned the attic into a master suite, creating an upstairs where every bedroom had its own bath. He rented out the rooms for a year until he met his Sweet Wife; after that he started a family and they all used the big house in high style, everyone having their own bathroom.

With the kids grown, Mudflap wanted to take advantage of his home's income property status and started renting out his house for short term rentals, riding the wave of the Airbnb tsunami.

The young over-zealous Zoning Officer filed a complaint with the health department, citing Mudflap had too many bedrooms for the septic system and one of the bedrooms was illegally installed.

The fact was the town code enforcement officer 32 years prior did not require approval by the health department for one simple bedroom, unless the foot print was being expanded.

Mudflap addressed the oversight with the health department, and was able to fight off the first attack of the Zoneman.

69

Mudflap intuitively went back to the zoning office and inquired about who had filed a complaint against him. Zoneman was questioned and confessed it was he who did the deed.

Then he tried to turn it around and said, "I did it for your best interest because you are in violation of rental laws, and I want you to become a formal Bed and Breakfast, but first you had to pass with the health department."

Zoneman told Mudflap there was a law against short-term rentals in New Hartford and he was not allowed to operate his income property without a long-term lease.

Right away Mudflap questioned the rule and the town's ability to dictate lease terms. Zoneman said, "You must become a Bed and Breakfast to conform to the laws." He had a dream of what the town should be like, a perfect little downtown world with everything in high order. He was looking way up in the sky, high in the "Ozone of a Utopia."

Mudflap just wanted to rent his house short term, not be a breakfast place, too. The food service creates another whole world of chores and issues. Bed and Breakfast places fall into other laws and guidelines, too, that Mudflap didn't want to get involved with.

Remember, little New Hartford is small and is an in-between town struggling with growth.

Ozone-Man wanted New Hartford to be like the upscale towns and regulate everything; he especially hated Airbnb. With no ability to control them, he thought Mudflap was a soft target and he decided to make Mudflap conform to the standards of his Utopia that was not yet written into the zoning laws.

Mudflap at first did not question Ozoneman's word quoting the law. He cooperated and paid to file for a variance and scheduled a hearing. Mudflap did make an issue of the breakfast service and told Ozoneman he did not serve food and was not comfortable with the issue.

Ozone took it upon himself to white out Mudflap's request for short-term rentals on the variance. He changed the paperwork and demanded Mudflap include food service in the request and again quoted law to Mudflap, with a biting edge of language, stating in a bullying fashion, "I don't want to have to shut you down". Mudflap was taken aback and just kept playing along.

First the health department complaint and Ozone fires out rule of law, then the threats of closing Mudflap's income property, all because Mudflap had questions trying to help the Economic Development Board.

That's what I call Economic Discouragement ! ! !

Playing Good Ozone, Bad Ozone, simultaneously, he told Mudflap that he did not have to attend the request for variance hearing and that Ozone himself would be there to go to bat for Mudflap and help him through the process of becoming legal.

Ozone came back from the sky with demands from the gods of Zoning. They wanted completely new plans from a Surveyor, an Architect and an Engineer, even though there was no new construction or any changes being made to the property at all. The survey and the plot plan filed in the town's records were not good enough; the house which has been

71

there for 120 years was in question of absolutely everything. The gods wanted $10,000+ worth of professional designs.

The survey demand especially bothered Mudflap because he was not doing anything at all with the property line and the request for a survey was coming from one of the Zoning gods who was himself a Surveyor. That fact and demand Mudflap thought fell directly into the issue of "conflict of interest."

Mudflap had enough of the bullying and called up the selectman's office and asked to speak to the Sensible Voice of Reason. He was very supportive to Mudflap and said, "I think you're right. Those demands sound a little overkill to me. I will help you with a plan that will not cost you so much (he had formally been a professional appraiser). But I think you may deserve a pass on the whole thing since you are an income property already. Check the ordinances again to be sure. Remember, knowledge is power."

That statement stuck with Mudflap and it kept rolling in his mind, "knowledge is power."

Luckily for Mudflap, all this was happening during his January-March writing time that was his new focus. After 40+ years of fighting and working through the winters, he felt the need for a change up.

Mudflap's time off was coming to a close, his money was running out, and the hype of the virus was spreading making everyone more and more anxious. This whole thing of Ozone "shutting down his rental property" was really starting to stress him out.

He went back to Ozone in person because he was not responding to the emails Mudflap sent in protest to the Zoning

Gods' demands. He asked about the local town ordinances and where did it dictate time limits of income properties?

Mudflap was now on the offensive and told Ozone he had the support of the Selectman and gave him an overview of their discussion. He wanted to know more about the town ordinances.

Ozone looked very uncomfortable and said, "Well, there's no town law, it's a state law." Mudflap saw a flash of fear in his countenance as he made the statement. Then Ozone started to talk of "Laws against Transients." He was making people in transition sound like vermin that should be fought off. "The State does not like transitional people," he said. He then changed the subject to the application and made some suggestions and said again, "I am trying to help you. I want to see your property legally operating. I don't want to have to shut you down."

Every time he said "shutdown" Mudflap felt threatened and he does not respond well to threats; so, with the Sensible Voice of Reason in his head saying, "knowledge is power," he went back home to Sweet Wife and had her help him research the State laws.

Ozone had called the Airbnbs a "cluster ^%#@ that is out of control and needs to be addressed." And part of the problem was that Mudflap had gotten involved with them and had put himself in a bad position.

Mudflap himself swears like a drunken sailor but edits himself in front of women. He noticed the secretary in the office when Ozone swore, looked over and said, "Careful of those tender ears." He asked her if she had heard that and she seemed to come out of a preoccupied daze and said, "What?" like she had been deaf. Prior though, she had made comments

73

on other issues. Funny how the town office works with selected hearing and opinions.

As Sweet Wife helped in the research of the State laws, it became apparent that there was no law against transitional people or rental agreements.

He went back again to Ozone and confronted him. Mudflap was now mad that he had been lied to twice, first about Town law and second about State law; and now he was questioning the friendly help Ozone was offering to make him legal.

Ozone didn't want to back down and fired his biggest gun off that he was keeping in reserve. He threatened Mudflap with The Town Lawyer. He started talking about already having consulted with The Lawyer and that a judgement had been made already on Mudflap's case.

Mudflap was in violation of "Transient Law." Ozone once again bullied Mudflap and simultaneously said, "I am on your side, and I want to help you."

Mudflap went back to double check his research and fired off another email, not only rebuffing Ozone's view of the law, but of what he felt about the Zoning Gods.

Ozone never replied to any of Mudflap's emails, so he kept going into the town offices. He had Crystal in the loop, relaying information to the Selectman. Mudflap, having lake properties and islands in highly regulated zones, was acutely aware of how zoning restrictions were spelled out, clearly stating intent of use. The rules did not need a lawyer to figure out the nuance of the language.

Mudflap called Ozone and was now totally on the offensive, unafraid of the lawyer threat. He was on a roll, like a predator smelling fear in the herd, he was on him. Ozone the Bully cried, "foul" and interrupted Mudflap's call, handing it over to Crystal and told her with a whiny little cry, "He's attacking me!" As much as Mudflap loves Crystal, he stood his ground and debated with her the issues he had.

Mudflap was now totally pissed off and eager to fight all the way to court. The State had no laws against "transients" or stopping income properties from short-term rentals. In reality, the State is in partnership with Airbnb, collecting taxes directly from the internet company. Mudflap also found out that Bed and Breakfast places only pay 11% tax instead of 15% to the State; Ozone's plan was going to short the State's taxes.

He now viewed the State as an Ally in the fight against the Zoning Gods, the Lawyer, and the little Demi-God Bully, Ozone.

Mudflap's mind was totally made up, his anger and resolve so focused that the powers that be in the Town Hall felt that resolve.

Somewhere out in the clouds of the ozone, out in "Olympus," the Gods heard the Sensible Voice of Reason and decided to drop their case against Mudflap.

When he came back to confront Ozone, he found a humbled, wounded Demi-God drowned by the cold waters of reality and offering total capitulation.

Trying to save some face, he offered up a piece of paper showing the State may at some point make Mudflap pay a special yearly fee regarding short-term rentals. He went on about some bill that may pass in the future but had already died in committee; he even went as far as to apologize for his overzealous actions.

In Mudflap's emails he demanded that Ozone go back to Olympus and the Gods and correct his mistake in the formal minutes of the meeting. Mudflap wanted it perfectly clear he was not in any violation of law concerning renting his home. Ozone, who at first absolutely refused to correct his mistake formally, was now more receptive. Mudflap said, "You can do it yourself and put it the way you want or I will make a statement to the Gods and you may not like what I have to say."

Mudflap came home to Sweet Wife waving the paper from Ozone. Channeling history, he stated as he waved the paper at her, "Peace in our time," like Chamberlin after his meeting with Hitler. Because that's just about as much as Mudflap trusts Ozone.

Mudflap planned on attending the next meeting in Olympus to witness the complete capitulation of Ozone and his "Failed Blitz." He intended to make some statement, too, but would go easy on the little wounded demi-god. Mudflap looked forward to looking at all the Gods in their eyes.

But the whole thing is on stall here in Real Time; all town meetings except the Selectmen's are cancelled, along with every public gathering and businesses of all sorts as the "Coronavirus" sweeps America.

Every time Mudflap thinks of the Gods of Olympus and the wounded Demi-God, a tune plays in his head: Commander Cody and his Lost Planet Airmen's song, "Lost in the Ozone"

"I'm lost in the Ozone again."
"I'm lost in the Ozone again."
"One drink of wine, two drinks of gin"
"and I'm lost in the Ozone again."
"Yee Ha!"

At the last minute the Selectmen's meeting was cancelled, too.

Mudflap presses onward,
Over and Out !

Jay Alden Bailey

What's Right or Wrong ?

The answer is not always clear.

Bullies for the most part should be simply avoided but sometimes you can't. And when your back is against the wall, or you have the opportunity to act in someone's behalf, turning a blind-eye is not necessarily the best course of action.

You can only let things slide off you for so long and even though it's much better to ignore Bullies and problem people, at some point a person has to stand their ground and defend themselves because there is not always a Mudflap there for you.

It's easier to run from problems, but it can be toxic to your being to let yourself be a victim; it's much harder standing up to any overwhelming force. Throughout history, those who stand against oppression and/or fight, with the odds stacked against them, become our legendary heroes.

Confronting a bully is more about your own redemption and seeking reprisal and reconciliation for the value of your self-image. If you can get the bully to show any form of remorse, maybe they will think twice before forcing their will upon another again.

Laughter is a great weapon, so very sharp it slices deep into the thin skin of a Bully's ego.

Note: When handling arms of any kind, be careful not to hurt yourself. Keep your powder dry and watch out for backfires.

Stand up for what you believe and fight.
Mudflap, Over and Out !

CHAPTER 3

BULLIES AND OTHER PESTS

Pick your battles well.
Mudflap, Over and Out !

(The First Book's Cliffhanger)

(Bowerbank, Maine)

Let's start with Captain Troll and sweep this pest out of the way so we can go on to more important matters. Mudflap likes shortcuts.

After living his Vacationland Hell for over a decade, Mudflap is done with this guy and just wants to move on quickly as possible.

A re-cap for past readers and to bring my new readers up to speed:

The Captain is a big Bully who retired from his shipping career and purchased a lake property that Mudflap has a deeded "right of way" through to access his home on the Phoebe Island.

With nobody to shout orders at, his deflated ego, combined with selfishness and greed, inspired the Captain to focus a campaign of harassment against Mudflap for well over a decade.

Unable to control himself, his anger grew and he turned to threats of physical violence. Then the Captain went to a very bad place, a big "social faux pas" of our times; he said, "I have the right to shoot you because you're on my land."

We last left Mudflap burnt out with the Captain's harassment, tired of all the work trips, and the seven-hour drives, too. Heartbroken by the loss of his puppy who died at the Island and was buried up by Mudflap's pond. To top it off, he was struggling through it all with an exploding hernia pushing through his gut.

Mudflap contacted a realtor; he listed the Island and his land with the ponds. The Captain had the nerve to call up the realtor and tell them not to advertise the Island with a right of way to shore. Then he obstructed the right of way with his boat trailer, too, discouraging buyers.

Captain Troll didn't want Mudflap to sell; he wanted to trap him there and harass him more, his actions becoming plain madness.

Mudflap takes his gloves off.
Over and Out !

In War, there are Allies.

Friends of Friends and Enemies of Enemies.

Pick sides well, your place in history depends on it.

Mudflap, Over and Out !

After 60 years of being "thrown under the bus", Mudflap became self-aware.

The Old Tree Cutter had the breaks slammed on him by his hernia surgery. Facing a 12-week recovery period with the inability to lift anything, he had time to reflect on his life and mentally change it.

The author/facilitator awoke inside him.

The character "Mudflap," who had been there all along, came up to the surface. He has in the past battled, and in the future, will battle bullies and defend those in need.

Mudflap loves this quote: "Bullies are scared people hiding inside scary people."

It fits the Captain oh so well.

He got this quote from Michelle Obama. After finishing his selected summer reads, Mudflap was looking for something good to top off his Island time and stumbled on her book in the pile his Sweet Wife had brought along.

Funny how extremists have such narrow views. When Mudflap told his right-wing, author-group friend that he was reading Michelle's book, the man was shocked and even a bit enraged.

How can anyone learn or grow if they only experience one side of a viewpoint or only hang around with people who agree with them all the time? (See Prologue)

Let's finish business with the boor Captain Troll and the boring Phoebe Island Road Clan.

Mudflap is done with this crowd and, like Anthony in the Twilight Zone, he "wishes them away into the corn."

In anticipation of trouble to come in the next season, Mudflap made a formal complaint to the Sheriff's department and headed off the Captain's campaign of harassment.

Mudflap and Wife arrived in Bowerbank without their usual pontoon boat loaded with supplies. Instead, they were sporting a construction trailer full of aluminum wheel-chair ramps, railings and platforms to upgrade their dock/walkway to the Phoebe Island.

Alone now and having no children in tow, the couple went about their business of opening up the Island home in a slower and more moderate pace, reflecting their age and maturity.

Right away, the first encounter they had was with the Good Neighbor who is a year-round, local Maine resident. He was always neutral, never taking sides, and for years was an advocate of minding your own business.

Sadly, he turned to the dark side and allied himself with the Captain in the Blockade of 2018 and that season's harassment of Mudflap and family.

(He must have found it easier to appease Captain Troll who lives there half the year, rather than side with the Mudflaps who are only around for a few weeks.)

The other Phoebe Island Road resident is a Flatlander or Person from Away; the Captain's little buddy, "ally in mischief and abuse," I dub "Gilligan."

The Good Neighbor met the couple passing by and immediately gave Mudflap a reprimand about being a bad neighbor for calling the sheriff on the Captain. He was going on about how hurtful and unneighborly Mudflap was for doing so. As he went on, he stuck his foot further and further into his mouth. He said, "So he makes a few idle threats and takes some rocks off your property for his wall, what's the big deal?"

Poor, poor little bully Captain Troll, his feelings are hurt, call a "Waambulance," he's having a crying attack.

Well, for one thing, threats of being shot for going to your lake house is completely off the wall. And secondly, the Captain's complete contempt by stealing from an abutting neighbor's land was way past a few rocks; he took a tractor and removed a very large boulder framing the entrance to Mudflap's driveway.

The Good Neighbor himself had just redone his home recently, and he paid big bucks for an elaborate wall to be built. If Mudflap took a tractor and removed one of his boulders, the man would go crazy.

Is it because Mudflap's property is less elaborate that his entrance has no value?

Mudflap changed the subject and told The Good One that he had written a book the past winter and that Bowerbank was in the book,

83

making his first sale of the 22 books Mudflap would continue to sell in the upcoming weeks.

Mudflap smiled and said, "You made the book, as well as a few others around here." The Good One's eyes widened, starting to get the picture.

But he couldn't get his foot out of his mouth and he said, "You have to put your big boy pants on and suck it up."

I don't think standing up to somebody who is threatening and bullying you around, stealing from your land, and disrespecting your entire family is wearing little boy pants or diapers.

The Good One kept digging himself deeper in a hole and made some "City Boy" remark.

(Here we go!) I tried to be nice.

He thinks he some woodsman because he's a recreational hunter and fisherman; but he spent his life as an office manager wearing nice shoes and a clean shirt. He puts on his cute, clean little L.L. Bean hunting jacket and is in a delusion that everybody below the northern New England states lives in a city.

Get this picture: When Mudflap arrives to open up his island house, he's in work clothes that are so badly ripped, stained and worn, with boots to match, that are so far gone, they are unfit to wear cutting trees and digging in the dirt at clients' houses.

While the Good One, local Mainer, is poking around his yard with cute, shiny shoes and shorts to match and in a perfectly clean polo shirt, Mudflap is going up and down the hill to the Island and back to his 22 acres on shore, hauling gear and docking equipment with a wheel barrel, dressed in rags.

Mr. Fancy Pants can't walk around his is 1-acre property and drives his ATV everywhere he goes.

He spends his life at a desk, while Mudflap spends his in the trees and he has the nerve to call him a "City Boy" and put on your "Big Boy Pants!" He keeps using the word Boy? He wouldn't make it to coffee time on a Mudflap tree job before he would be running home in tears.

Dogs' names in Mudflap's life evolve.   Like Susie, became Suzer, then the Poozer. Ellie became L, then L. Dog, then L-A-Doo, and finally Doo Dog. Lucy became LuLu and is now "The Lu."

Well, people's nick names evolve, too. Like, The Good Neighbor, into The Good One and then into Fancy Pants.

(And finally, just Fancy, because everything he has is so very perfect. A perfect big boat, perfect little boat, and a perfect dock. A perfect, polished tractor and perfect toys, all perfectly stored around his perfectly fancy house.)

On the fire department garage of Bowerbank, a sign reads, "The Edge of the Wilderness" on the only paved road in town; every other road is dirt. In the middle of the woods, Fancy, the guy who hates the city, has almost every inch of his front yard paved shiny black, like the Ace of Spades; perfectly asphalted right to the front door. A pine cone doesn't last 10 minutes and not one single green wisp of anything dares to grow. A perfect black stain in the beautiful woods, so dark and shiny it can be seen from space in the satellite pictures.

I got another picture for you: I don't know what the Sheriff said to the Captain, he wouldn't confide to Mudflap the details, but how would you feel if one of the most top officials of the County just happened to be in the neighborhood and thought he would drop by and see how things were going with you and your neighbor.

Whatever he said to him must have sunk in deep because Mudflap never saw the Captain up close for the entire month; the right of way stayed clear and no eye contact was made or one word was exchanged.

Good job, Sheriff, you're the hero!

Mudflap put his dock up in peace.

Five years rolls around fast as you age and it was Bowerbank Day again. Mudflap ran into Gilligan, who is always nice to your face and stabs you in the back first chance he gets. Mudflap told old Gilligan, in a happy, friendly way, about his new and improved dock; and mentioned he wasn't going to take it up and down anymore because he and the Mrs. plan to be in Bowerbank more often now that they are reaching close to their retirement.

Mudflap sells books to any neighbor he can except the Captain and Gilligan.

The month was a success: books read and sold, dock up and complete, fun and maintenance all done. Mudflap and Sweet Wife head back to Connecticut.

Within a matter of a few days, the blow back from the fire set off by the rage of The Phoebe Island Road Clan who hate Phoebe Island, reached 400 miles back to Connecticut.

Complaints, and demands that the dock must be removed from the Island, were spearheaded by Gilligan, who holds some volunteer position for the town. (As soon as your back is turned, he is there with the knife.) He also was a spear-tip for pushing the new ordinance laws that the locals had to shoot down.

Gilligan, the Captain, and Fancy made formal complaints and demands to the town and state, insisting Mudflap had no rights to a dock, citing that it was not in his deed.

Docks are not a deeded right. They are a use granted by the state and everyone on the lakes have the same privileges.

The book really didn't tell anybody in Bowerbank anything new, the Captain already had a reputation of abuse not only focused on Mudflap but to other folks in town as well; everybody who knows Gilligan is aware of his style, too. They respect each other's privacy but don't let that make you think anything gets by them; the locals are a sharp group.

The three Bullies have shamed themselves in the eyes of the true, liberty-loving conservatives in the sweet little town of Bowerbank, home of the free, the brave, the fair, and the decent.

Ya gotta love 'em.
Mudflap, Over and Out !

P.S. Real Time: Summer 2020, petty drama from the Clan.

Sweet Wife said, "I haven't seen any bears in Bowerbank, but there are plenty of boors around."

Bullies and Pests:

The only difference is their size, or are they the same?

Mudflap, Over and Out !

Maine and Up Country

(Haul them in and keep 'em tied up.)

Most times, when you hear laughter, someone's the brunt of the joke and it's a form of Bullying.

Funny how in Maine, Vermont, and New Hampshire, their Flatlander and People-from-Away jokes can have a bullying edge to the humor; but there is a bias pass given to women, an unfair sexist attitude.

Not only do the locals look more kindly on Women from Away, they go as far as to import them and acclimate these women into their society. Mudflap knows personally women that have been imported from all over southern New England as well as Pennsylvania, New Jersey, Virginia and California. In Maine, he has met women from South Africa and Tasmania.

Mudflap was surprised to find out that some of these women were transplants because they were so very well ingrained into the community that they had developed their own disdain of Flatlanders.

Governor LePage of Maine once made a horrible statement that originally offended Mudflap. He said, "We have to watch out for the men of Connecticut. They bring in drugs and impregnate our women."

Upon further reflection, Mudflap had to agree with LePage. Many Connecticut guys do party hard and it's very likely they would bring drugs into the State. And if Maine men would take better care of their own women, the Connecticut guys wouldn't have to pick up the slack and knock them up.

MF. Over and Out !

West Hartford Connecticut

(The cost of independence)

There is a lady dog walker in Mudflap's tree-working neighborhood, who was hitting heavy on him. Women have a sexual advantage over men that cannot be denied. He tried to keep polite and play along without getting in too deep.

She asked for assistance on her property with her trees and Mudflap went to do an estimate for her. Her questions turned personal and she grilled him for information. Mudflap played along, trying not to overstep his bounds and kept things professional.

She asked question after question as they walked around the property. Mudflap evaluated her landscape and her motives. She invited him inside to check her calendar and exchange information; the home was very up scale, way beyond the means of a dog walker. Her questions kept getting more personal and by her countenance Mudflap could tell she was beginning to get a little frustrated that he was not asking more personal questions in response.

She started to offer up her own information, such as her divorced status, golf club membership and so on. She invited him to the club for a meal. Mudflap declined saying, "I know a lot of people in that club. I have a lot of friends there and we get along well, but I'm the hired help. They pay a lot of money not to drink with guys like me."

"That's ridiculous," she said. "Oh no, it's not," replied Mudflap. "There is a reason I don't live here in West Hartford." She was starting to get real antsy and Mudflap was losing patience with the game. He started thinking he didn't want the job and she was becoming a Pest.

90

Finally, she said, "All you do is talk about yourself and you know nothing about me!"

"Well," said Mudflap, "I know somebody paid a lot of money to get rid of you."

Oh, my! That widened her eyes and Mudflap saw a very similar look, just like his brother used to have right before he started swinging punches.

Mudflap still sees her regularly, walking the dogs in many neighborhoods and he is as nice as he can be. After he wrote his first book, he mentioned it to her as she walked by and she replied, "I have heard all about it. I guess you don't want to be a tree guy anymore." Not only did she not want a book but she was extremely mean about it, saying bad and negative things.

She picks up crap and talks crap, too.
MF. Over and Out !

Jay Alden Bailey

Who's on first?
Remember Abbot and Costello?

Marriage can be a Comedy Team,
and a Tag Team, too!

Mudflap, Over and Out !

West Hartford, Connecticut

(Chain of Command)

The Little General is how her husband describes her. A humorous way to say she is first in charge. Mudflap has been taking orders from The Little General for 25 years and is dedicated to her in service and loyalty.

Often spouses play a good-cop, bad-cop routine; one buddies up, the other cracks the whip and makes demands. Mudflap is aware and realizes it is regular business; spouses are a team and should be on the same side. Often, it's the Yin and Yang thing playing out, too. A good service person understands this. And to be successful and survive the encounter with some skin left, one must cater to both and bring them into the middle of things.

In the end the best people focus on quality and the demands and whip cracking lessen. Mudflap has found that even the toughest in the crowd ease up on their service people as their loyalty is proven over the years. The quality of the master shows through in response to the quality of the service they receive.

But in reverse, the lack of quality shows through and sometimes the "Little Generals" of the world give away their position and get flanked; they lose their ranks' respect and support.

Mudflap is old school. Despite the high-tech world, he still spends the time to personally stop and check his yards, catering to the whims of his loyal clients in person. He doesn't like the text and click world where clients expect their service people to snap to it with the push of a button.

Especially irritating are the unknown shopping customers, who tag trees with ribbons and leave messages or texts and expect prices without even a moment of personal interaction. These types of people are almost never satisfied and have some issue or big problem at the end of the job.

There are factors that cause good clients to go to a begrudging place when paying for service.
1st) The sale of their home: once they decide to list the property they detach, period.
2nd) College: Mudflap has many times taken the hit when the kids go off to school.
3rd) Any budget crisis or large expenditure: the yard must take a back seat. Mudflap has been cancelled for all sorts of things. Worst of all, when they reschedule, the whip comes out and the crew must push extra hard to make up for lost time.
4th) Vacations: the last and most irritating reason to let the property go.

Mudflap doesn't care what high-end school the kids go to, or what exotic place is on the vacation schedule. He only cares about the quality of the property and keeping up with the chores.

The Little General flew off to France and blew a big wad of cash. Twenty-five years of loyal service meant nothing to her. Mudflap was cancelled with a cold text and no reply to his return call.

She mentioned something about catching up in the spring.

Not a chance in Hell !
MF. Over and Out !

West Hartford, Connecticut

(Jekyll and Hyde)

Once, very long ago, when Mudflap was a young and naive contractor, he experienced an extreme version of the good-spouse, bad-spouse tag team.

Mudflap did a complicated large-tree removal, between a house and garage with a deck built around the giant trunk; a job that today he would recommend to a crane company.

The gentleman he made the deal with was a mild-mannered, rotund fellow, with a sweet smile, grey and balding, sporting heavy, black-rimmed glasses.

The cut tree tops were piled high to the edge of the deck to save it from being smashed by the trunk. It had been a horrible task and the crew was tired. They were eager to drop the trunk onto the pile as it was the last chore of the day, and everyone wanted to go home.

Abruptly, the wife came out. She looked like some old-world Madonna figure clothed in a long black dress, like out of some 200-year-old Catholic Church painting. She stopped the job and everyone had to stand around and watch as she knelt at the tree's base and cried uncontrollably for a very long time.

Finally, the husband came out to rescue the crew from the distraught wife and got her out of the way. They dropped the trunk and the young men got off the property quickly, eager to hit the liquor store.

The next day they came back to finish up the job. All went well and it was time to get paid and go home. As the tools were being packed up the gentleman came out with checkbook in hand and approached the crew. They all were stunned by his appearance. He had lost the glasses and was much better dressed. No longer bald, he had on a toupee and had lost his sweet smile, too.

He was much more assertive and had a scowl that could take down a librarian. He demanded a discount off the work due to his wife's unhappiness with damage done to the lawn. Bad enough that she had lost the tree, but the thin, poorly kept lawn had to be reseeded, and she was very distraught, again.

The men could see her at the door watching, handkerchief to her eyes. They looked back at the gentleman, over to Mudflap and to each other. Everyone was in shock taking in the bizarre scene.

Mudflap stood his ground. The job was done well and the grass was the least of the worries. The deck didn't have a scratch on it and the clean-up was perfect. But it still took a half hour of arguing before he got paid.

Finally, the young crew got out of there. First stop was the liquor store.

MF. Over and Out !

Neighbors

**You got to live with them.
But you could live without them.**

Welcome to the Neighborhood.

When you are new, get off on the right foot.

Mudflap, Over and Out !

New Hartford, Connecticut

In the first book, Mudflap was attacked and ganged up on by the whole neighborhood of the Laurel Beach Association on West Hill, just for building a garage.

When a new neighbor moved in, Mudflap went to a zoning variance hearing to speak up on her behalf, defending her against the small-minded association who not only abused him but gave other people hard times over building projects, too.

A few years later, Mudflap was working in his yard dumping chips for mulch. This same neighbor lady, whom Mudflap had defended earlier, approached him with questions saying, "Is this legal? Can you dump these chips?"

"Legal?" said Mudflap. "Don't you remember that I'm your friend? I spoke up for you at the zoning hearing when you wanted to expand your garage."

98

Well, that didn't seem to carry any weight and she continued to keep yipping at him. Then she threatened to call and report him to the town; another "Little General." Mudflap said, "Listen, Sweetheart, you're confused. Don't come on my property when I'm doing maintenance, threaten me, and tell me what I can or can't do." She then said, "You know ladies over 50 don't like to be called Sweetheart." "I know, Sweetheart," said Mudflap. "Move along now."

Coincidently, just a week earlier, Mudflap had trouble from the new owners of the cottage across from the same side where the Sweetheart lived. The prior owners had caused trouble before, so Mudflap was sensitive to this part of his land.

The previous owners, when renovating the cottage, used Mudflap's property to park trucks and hauled demolition garbage into his yard. Where do people get the nerve to treat their neighbors like that?

So, Mudflap is driving down the road, and he sees a SUV truck parked totally in the middle of his yard. He stops and watches the new neighbors moving furniture into their cottage. He goes over and says, "Do you always park on people's lawns like that?" and points at their truck. "Well, not usually," she said.

Mudflap gets it, their driveway is limited and his yard is so open and all nicely mowed. It's just so tempting and convenient to use his property.

The very first thing she does when she moves into a new neighborhood is park in the middle of the neighbor's lawn? Really? How rude and inconsiderate could a person possibly be? Not someone Mudflap wants to live next to.

So, Mudflap told her, "If you wouldn't do it where you come from then don't start doing it here. Get your vehicle off my lawn!" and then he added, "Oh, by the way. Welcome to the neighborhood, Sweetheart."

The next day he installed two pipes, as posts, straddling the opening of his side yard. He roped it off, hanging orange streamers all down the line; not exactly the nicest view, but she should have thought twice before plowing into a new neighborhood and doing what she damn well pleased.

Mudflap's advice is:
As a newcomer, get to know your neighbor first, before you start taking liberties.
Over and Out !

P.S. Real Time, Mudflap spent mid-January through mid-March writing *Mudflap II*. He was up at 4:30 to 5:30 am, working on the book till noon. Then spent his afternoons chasing small boats and canoes he found for sale online. His goal was to get some boats for his daughter's yoga retreats at the Sebec Lake camp in Maine. The extra canoes and boats he bought were to pay for the yoga retreats' boats with sales and maybe put a few bucks in Mudflap's pocket, too.

You know Mudflap, when he goes, he goes all out. And he bought too many boats to store on Main Street. His high traffic spot on the State highway was his focus for sales but his property on West Hill near the Lake could get him some action, too.

So, Mudflap has boats for sale on his side lawn, across from The Two Sweethearts. I am sure they are going to love it. If they don't like the look of the boats, he has some blue tarps ready to improve the view.

What kinda action will Mudflap get is the question? Will the Sweethearts complain to the town? Will a complaint fall on Ozone's desk?

Mudflap has had an Antiques and Collectibles sign on Main Street for over a decade. His first sign included Custom Cannons (black-powder, full-scale replica barrels) for re-enactments, 4th of July and other fair-weather events. He combined his love of history and antiques and got into military collectibles with his son, too. Well, Sandy Hook sure took the fun out of guns in Connecticut and some seriously restrictive laws were passed. Mudflap, in step with the times, was no longer interested is selling guns to anyone and changed his sign to just Antiques and Collectibles.

When he started renting out his house, he changed the sign again to an understated business titled The West End.

His idea was to include his rental property with any and all business he may want to conduct on his Main Street location. You don't really know what The West End is, it's just a title; could be anything.

During the battle with the Demi-God Ozone, Mudflap did discuss with him his right to conduct business and retail sales on Main Street. Ozone said, "You're not zoned retail." Mudflap said, "I went through the formal permission process for the signage, had to contact the neighbors and everything. I am approved for retail." Ozone was not so sure but said he had no problem with boat sales, as long as there were some breaks in the display action.

The bigger issue was the rental of Mudflap's home and Ozone's desire for him to become a full-service Bed and Breakfast. So, at the time, Mudflap didn't discuss further the retail sales subject with Ozone.

Mudflap waited a couple days after the capitulation of Ozone and his Failed Blitz. Then he put the biggest boat he had acquired for sale out in his front yard. Mudflap figured once that boat sold everything else would be a de-escalation of boat displays, rather than the reverse.

Mudflap really is a most reasonable fellow to deal with; but he's digging his heels in and is not about to lose ground as he keeps following Ozone's retreat. He has not had his moment in the presence of the Gods of Olympus. With no meetings scheduled in the foreseeable future because of the pandemic, no business is being conducted, especially town meetings, as these volunteer gods are all very old and in the high-risk group for virus complications.

The spring market for the whole nation and the world is under attack.

The Coronavirus has changed everything. The brakes are on the whole economy and people's outlook on life in general has changed dramatically. The Sunday morning news showed cruise ships sequestered offshore of Florida, lined up like in a parking lot.

Fear and crisis once again take the front seat of not only America but of the world. We go from terrorists to shooters, then to stock markets; it's a non-stop waterfall of crap. Now this virus thing will have the most lasting effect of all. It's a terrorist we can't see and will never go away. Hopefully, it will just slip into the background like AIDS did once there is a vaccine.

Mudflap tried to be upbeat and fight the depressing feeling entrapping everyone. He put a sign on a cute, little blue boat that said, "Be Happy."

But will they get the message? Did Ozone get the message? Did he get the memo? Mudflap is a good person to just leave alone.

A jingle from Commander Mudflap and his Lost Planet Tree-Men: Lost !

"I'm lost in the Ozone again."
"Yes, lost in the Ozone again."
"Oh, Baby, lost."
"Oh, Sweetheart, lost."
"Oh, yeah, now Everybody lost."
"Yes, we're All lost in the Ozone again."
"Yeee Haa ! "

MF. In defiance of the Little Bullies and Pests, Out !

P.P.S. Real Time: Zoom meetings start in all sorts of different venues but they just aren't the same as the personal interactions. Mudflap is taking a break from Town meetings, still taking the time to read the minutes and stay abreast of things.

MF.

If you have a problem, don't threaten your neighbors with the authorities.

And don't call the town or police behind their backs either. (Unless they are threatening to kill you.)

Mudflap, Over and Out !

New Hartford, Connecticut

(So, who really is a Good Neighbor?)

Mudflap likes the quaint old homes on the Main Street where he lives and he likes the state highway's high visibility for the sale of items, too. Often the Main Street homes have tag sales or cars to sell by the roadside. These activities don't detract from the charm of the neighborhood but there is a limit.

Mudflap takes extra good care of his property because he has had neighbors complain to the town about him many times before for all sorts of different things. So, Mudflap keeps the best-kept yard around, not only for himself, but to keep the criticism down, too.

When the house across the street changed hands, the new neighbors started taking advantage of the high visibility spot. They started selling cars and having tag sales. It was not a problem and for the longest time Mudflap just ignored the piles of stuff.

Mudflap's patience was thinning, even though he keeps a lot of things around, and likes a sale item at the street, too. The one car after another for sale didn't bother him, or the regular tag sales; the killer was the pile of tires that never went away. If they sold one pile, the next pile was moved out.

Mudflap had been abused by his neighbors for trucks in his back yard and for building a garage to keep things neat and put away. They have shot his dogs and threatened to shoot him for passing by to his lake house. Neighbors can be crazy. Mudflap likes to be left alone and does the same to others. But even in the shaggiest of neighborhoods, never mind the upscale quaint ones, does anybody want to see piles of tires in the front yard, permanently?

Mudflap won't call the cops or the town on a neighbor. He will just say something, let the neighbor know his opinion and try to be polite about it.

Mudflap asked the neighbor to tone it down a bit, especially the tire thing. Well, Mr.Tire Pile got mad, his wife gave Mudflap a smack on the shoulder, and shoved him with a scream. Mudflap let it go and walked away.

A few days later he heard about his visit from a town cop. He was surprised to hear there was a complaint. Mudflap said, "Gee, somebody called you? She's the one who got rough and started shoving me around."

The cop said, "Why didn't you report her?" Mudflap replied with a chuckle, "Come on, Dan, do you think I'm going to come crying to you that my neighbor lady hit me? Come on, really? I got more dignity than that."

Mudflap, Mr.Tire Pile and his wife are friendly now. They got the idea and have a nice yard. It didn't take the town or the police to get it across.

Another neighbor on Main Street liked to let his dogs out at 5:30 am every morning and the first thing they did was start non-stop barking for a least 10 to 15 minutes. This went on for years. One spring morning, the first night Mudflap left the window open, they woke him up. You know that last half hour of sleep that's so valuable, those slumbering moments? Well, nobody wants to hear a dog barking non-stop.

Mudflap woke up with a swear on his lips and said to his wife, "I'm calling Joe, we can't listen to this every morning till next winter." She protested, but later in the day Mudflap left him a message and said, "The whole neighborhood is tired of waking up to your dogs," and hung up. (Mudflap had been talking to the abutting homeowner on the other side of Joe who had been gritting his teeth for years, too.)

Mudflap received a nasty message in reply; Joe went off saying, "How do you know it's my dogs? There are other dogs in the neighborhood, why are you calling me?" He went on and on and at the end of the message he said, "I will keep them quiet."

That made Mudflap laugh. Good one Joe, and he has been keeping his promise, too.

Unless your neighbor is threatening to kill you, don't call the cops, the town or the dog warden.

Don't threaten them with the authorities, just let them know how you feel, that's being a good neighbor.

Mudflap, Over and Out !

House builders are like car salesmen.
They will tell you anything to get you to sign.

You surprised?

Mudflap, Over and Out !

Canton, Connecticut

(Neighbors can stink)

There was this sanitation contractor who followed all the rules and had an upscale operation in a commercial/industrial zone. He was one of the biggest tax payers in his town.

Unlike Mudflap and other small contractors who push the limits and operate out of their residences. Complaining neighbors do have some justification when the contractors' yards get too messy.

An up-scale housing development was built behind the large, legitimate sanitation contractor.

This company had rows of septic tank pumpers, excavators of all kinds, and a huge assortment of trucks and other equipment, as well as a lot of portable outhouses.

The builder of these upscale homes assured the buyers that the company could not expand their operation, outright lied to them, making assurances that he had no right to make.

The huge operation had an undersized, outdated service garage and wanted to build a proper service center for the operation.

All the neighbors ganged up on this most reputable company owned by a life-long businessman who payed huge taxes to be in a legitimate location.

They cried about the look of the parking lot full of port-a-potties, the smell of the pump trucks, and the noise of the operation.

Nobody forced them to buy those homes; they knew what they were buying next to.

The rich neighbors used their combined money to hire lawyers and bully the owner, causing him ten years of grief and over $150,000 fighting to build his garage.

The reality was the port-a-potties were all very clean, the operation kept regular hours, and was not too noisy or didn't really smell bad.

The garage was built and the losing bullies cried like babies.

In the end, it was the rich neighbor bullies who were stinky and made all the noise.

MF. Over and Out!

MUDFLAP SHORTS:

Sometimes you just got to get on with things!

MF. Over and Out !

(Having money can change the way things are viewed.)

In Naples, Maine, a rich developer buys land on the Muddy River and changes the name to "Sebago Harbor Shores."

In West Hartford, Connecticut, there is a high-end retirement community called The Reservoir, but it's really across from "The Waste Treatment Plant."

MF. Out !

Connecticut

(The spiritual advisor.)

He thinks he's Christ the Angel, but he's really Chris the Devil.

Time changes your perspective on many things; one being, the older people that you may have looked up to when you were little seem to be a lot less impressive as you gain experience.

Mudflap admired his Brother's older and supposedly wiser friend who later in life fancied himself a minister of sorts. He was always preaching philosophy and going as far to perform the nuptial services at Mudflap's Brother's wedding.

Mudflap called him many years later when he felt a deep concern for his Brother's emotional well-being, hoping the Minister would somehow help his long-time friend.

The Minister was dismissive and tuned Mudflap out.

Not long after, the Brother's life ended at the bottom of the waterfall he had in his back yard.

After writing his first book, Mudflap contacted the Minister again. Coincidentally, he happened to be back in Connecticut, recuperating from a serious accident he had overseas on a vacation.

(Note: Beware vacations. They can be dangerous. People do things out of their regular routine of activities and there are many stories of serious vacation-time injuries.)

Jay Alden Bailey

Mudflap wanted the Minister to have a book, so he and his wife went to see him for a visit and to re-connect.

Mudflap took the time to cross the state, hoping for some closure to the past's tragedies. The Minister was more focused on his income property, having Mudflap do a tree evaluation at the re-connect.

He lives in Alaska now and has his brother watching over his income property in Connecticut. He told Mudflap a story about a dream he had -- water flowing and filling up his house. He called his brother and told him to check his property. Low and behold, the pipes had burst, but by his vast ESP connection he saved his house from a total disaster.

When he was through telling the story of his telepathy, Mudflap asked if he ever connected his phone call with the death of his Brother and his reply was, "No, it never struck me."

He was connected to his pockets and his own financial well-being through his vast ESP powers; he was feeling the water flowing in and his money flowing out.

But he couldn't feel his friend's life flowing out, even with the rush of a waterfall.

MF. Over and Out !

Alcohol is a sneaky drug.

A social drink is ok.

Alcohol is the worst drug of all because it's not only socially accepted, it can be socially expected.

(Death and divorce can be isolating experiences.)

Sometimes people just don't how to react to your grief with death and just avoid you, or judge you after divorce; these things ruin the good times and many people just don't want to deal with it all.

The same goes for quitting drinking. You're a drag and make people feel uncomfortable when you choose a clean drink. Thank, God, for designated drivers, gives the sober person a mission.

Mudflap was dry for 29 years until his daughter got him into craft beers. He enjoyed a two-year, after-work beer time. In the prior years, Sweet Wife always would say, "Sit on the porch and have a glass of wine or a beer." Mudflap never did, but once he started those beer times and would stop working and get nothing else done, Sweet Wife was not so happy about it.

After his surgery, the beer didn't agree with him anymore and he doesn't need the extra calories either. Being over 60 years old, Mudflap had to cut his meals in half, too. One has to adjust everything as they age.

Mudflap is dry again and is not as fun to hang out with, but Sweet Wife is happier, that's all that counts.

MF. Over and Out !

Contractors and Service People
Finance Advisors to Lawn Rakers

Friends, Heroes, Bullies and or Pests.

Mudflap's advice is:
Concentrate on quality.
Over and Out !

West Hartford, Connecticut

(Finance)

Money is power and everyone, from bankers to investors, anyone helping you with your money and financial future, can be a great asset or big problem; choose these people wisely.

When Mudflap started a family, many financial investor/insurance salesmen were on him like a cheap suit; the bullies came out in full force. When one guy questioned Mudflap and found out that he had a newborn, he enthusiastically said, "You have to protect them," and then he proceeded to try and sell him a big insurance package. He was ringing the wrong bell. Mudflap doesn't have to do anything he doesn't want to except pay taxes and die.

The advisors that hold back and don't push you are the people you want to deal with.

Another financial guy questioned Mudflap and found out he was pre-paying a 14% loan. He tried to stop him saying, "Don't pre-pay the loan. Use the interest as a tax write-off and I will make you 20% in the market."

Well, Mudflap figured by paying off the loan he was guaranteed the 14%, with no transaction fee, and he was reducing his liability, too.

He saw the advisor again a couple of years later and after another crash in the market; the changing times changed everything.

Mudflap said, "Hey, you know I saved your life a couple of years ago." The advisor looked at him with a questioning countenance.

Mudflap continued with a straight face (but laughing to himself) as he said, "If I listened to you, I would have lost everything and I would have had to kill you."

He replied with a little pout face, "I can't control the market." Well, that's not what he told Mudflap at the time.

Be careful of big promises.
MF. Over and Out !

Contractors

Find one you like personally.

Don't complain about anything, pay your bill, and shut up.

If you don't like something, just say redo it, don't make the money the issue, concentrate on the quality of the work.

Lastly, and most importantly, be loyal.

Happy Contractor, happy home environment, no leaks, no shorts, no messes.

Live with confidence.
MF. Over and Out !

Second Homes

Here is where you really must be careful of Bullies. Mudflap has owned property in and out of state (Maine) for over 30 years.

After three decades, Mudflap has current favorite contractors, all are excavators. In Winchester, Connecticut, Bowerbank, and Naples, Maine, too -- they are100% honest and hard working.

Also, his carpenter in Naples, Maine is a straight shooter and 99% on top of things. No carpenter is 100%, most are Prima Donnas. They prance around the job with inflated egos and overzealous ideas with no limit to what they think you can afford. It does not bother them at all how big your second mortgage will be when they are through.

Up country, every Darryl and Darryl story you ever heard is true. The more they need the job, the more likely they will be a problem for you. Don't let your generosity get the better of you. If you think you are doing them a favor hiring them, you are most likely to be headed for a disaster.

Hire people who don't need the work, period. And they can still become a problem, too, but for a different reason. Mostly it's out of their own convenience that they are working for you at all. Whether it's financial or physically convenient, or some other reason, the common denominator is still the same.

Just count on one thing, you are going to overpay no matter what; so just shut up and don't whine, it only makes it worse.

And whatever you do, pay well and don't complain, or you won't be happy with what you come back to.

Mudflap has been threatened many times, some threats more direct, others implied.

Be very careful of any perpetual maintenance, it won't be long before you're working for them.

If you have or want a second home, be ready to work on it yourself, pay through the nose and often do a combination of the two. If you can't handle it, rent a place, pay top dollar for the week, and save yourself all the aggravation.

Or just stay home and be happy.
MF. Over and Out !

Mechanics

Find one you like personally.

Don't complain about anything, pay your bill and shut up.

If you don't like something, just say redo it, don't make the money the issue, concentrate on the quality of the work and the safety of your vehicle.

Lastly and most importantly, be loyal.

Happy Mechanic, happy life.

Ride with confidence.
MF. Over and Out !

The Critic

She's famous, admired, respected. Her influence spans distance and time.

She's liked, loved, and most of all, she's feared.

She is Kate.

Don't mess with her.

Mudflap, Cautiously, Over and Out !

The Realtor's Poem

They beat up their sellers first;
then they beat up the buyers next.

They are cliquey and exclusive;
they click with the group and they click the mouse;
they click on line; they click their phones;
they click you on, they click you off;
they want to be paid with a click.

They will tell you anything for a listing or a sale,
hiding behind half-truths.

They want easy money fast, with little work;
and care nothing for all your many years of efforts.

They laugh and smile at a quick sale;
and cry and complain when it takes, too long.

They are the most selfish of Bullies;
preying on the old and the weak.

They want respect,
but give little in return.

They want it all now,
they want it all fast.

So, Good Luck with the realtors. You're going to need it.

If you find a good one, that needle in the proverbial haystack, keep them close, like your friends and your enemies !

MF> Out !

Islands and Boats in Real Estate.

Mudflap bought an Island cheap on the most exclusive lake in the State of Maine, because the realtors didn't want to bother with the boat ride and the extra effort it takes selling an Island.

He was originally told about the Island and was sent out by a realtor to check it out all alone.

In the new millennium, there has been an explosion of growth in Naples. Between the many marinas, accessories companies, and residential properties in the lake region of the Island, there must be 100 million dollars in boats and associated equipment.

Everybody pours out the money and thinks the boats are so fun and wonderful, riding around in joy-ride circles with nowhere really to go.

But when you want to sell an Island and ask a realtor and the buyers to take a boat ride, oh, God, get the binky out and start wiping up the tears.

MF.> Out !

Realtors

The Lazy, the Stupid, and the Dishonest.

Maine

(The Lazy)

Mudflap kept his Island in Naples' Long Lake off the market so it would not be a stale listing. He was ready to put it on for a good price and easy sale. He contacted "Prancy," the most senior broker in the highest profile office of the Lake Region. This broker had a cottage on the lake and a boat all ready to go, tied up at her dock.

Prancy promised Mudflap that she would personally be at any, and all, showings.

She got a buyer, but didn't want to bother going out herself and let the selling agent go out alone. Without guidance, the buyers were frustrated and made a disruptive mess of the property.

When Mudflap went out and saw the condition the unattended buyers left his Island in, and complained, wanting the name of the selling agent, he was told by Prancy that they had left the state with their buyers, were unavailable, and she didn't have their contact information.

He didn't believe that the agent had left the state; that was a completely fabricated story. If they were "Out of State Brokers" it would have been even more important not to let them go out alone. Not only was Prancy lazy, she was an out-right liar. (Caught three times, in case you lost count.)

Mudflap took the Island off again and waited; he wanted it back on with a proper fresh splash!

Mudflap The Gloves Come Off

Prancy sold her high-profile Sebago Lake Region brokerage; so, Mudflap thought some fresh blood, younger more-motivated agents would appreciate the listing and do a good job for him.

A two-women team wanted to take the property on and sounded all enthusiastic; so, Mudflap let them do their job without any micro-managing.

The write-up and pictures they chose for the cover were a disaster. Unbelievable, it was so bad.

The important features: Picnic and play games, enjoy the views and toast marshmallows.

They did not mention the 900+ feet of waterfront on the most exclusive lake in the state, or the close proximity to the famous and most popular hot spot in the whole region: the Naples Causeway, or the grandfathered house permitted to be expanded by 30%.

No, they wanted to advertise marshmallows.

The new splash was a belly flop. Mudflap took the Island off the market again and fired the "Marshmallow Twins."

MF. Disgusted, and Out !

Jay Alden Bailey

(The Stupid)

Mudflap once tried to sell his northern island in the Moosehead Lake Region and thought he would use a big experienced broker out of Bangor. The agent Wayne was a nice old fellow from the Newest Century Reality.

I will spare you the details and hit the punch line quick.

After the meeting, doing all the set-up work, papers, disclosures, etc., Mudflap went about his business and enjoyed the rest of his trip.

The agent went back to his office and did research on his own, not trusting Mudflap to be accurate with his disclosures. Mind you, this is an Island in one of the cleanest AA rated lakes in the whole state.

He stated, completely inaccurately, that the house was sided with "Asbestos Encapsulated in Vinyl."

When Mudflap got home to Connecticut and went online to see the listing, he hit the ceiling!

Calling the agent's boss, he explained the huge mistake and his concern about the long-term effect that information "online" would have on the property. Joe the head broker quickly took charge and did everything he could to erase the inaccurate disclosure from the Internet, with all the professional apologies possible.

Good job, Joe, another Mudflap of sorts, taking the heat for his help's stupidity.

The agent was a nice old guy but his IQ was Waning.

MF. Disillusioned, and Out !

(The Dishonest)

Back at the southern Island in Naples, another broker from the local area's Big Wind Bag of Hot Air Reality did a real shifty thing with Mudflap's listing.

Again, the Island was kept off for a while to make the listing fresh. Mudflap hired The Wind Bag and told him, "Now is the season to post my property."

The Wind Bag bragged about having a million-dollar island listing on Sebago lake, assuring Mudflap he was an island-selling guy.

Then, before listing it, he said, "Don't put the Island on the MLS at this time. There is a cheaper island then yours that just came on and it's going to hurt your sale."

Mudflap was not worried because his Island had a better location and he replied so. He told The Wind Bag to list the Island, period. Mudflap went about his business, disconnected from the Internet for his month-long trip to Maine. When he got back to Connecticut and went online, he couldn't find his listing.

Turns out, The Wind Bag took the contract but did not post the property on the MLS because he didn't want two Islands on the market competing with his million-dollar island. That was three times in a row that Mudflap left his property off the market to keep the listing fresh and three times in a row the realtors blew the re-listing and peak- season market.

Mudflap has more lazy, stupid, and dishonest realtor stories; there is no shortage of incompetence and bullies in the real estate world.

Mudflap, Overly Nauseous and Out !

More MF. Shorts:

Insurance

We all need peace of mind.

You can only count on Death, Taxes and somebody selling you Assurance.

New Hartford

(The Mean Girls Insurance)

They are The Baker Agency, selling you sweet savings treats and service muffins to draw you in. Then shove humble pie down your throat to keep you where they want you.

They are all sweet and nice when taking the business away from other agencies, promising to review your policies annually and keep saving you money.

As time passes, the rates go up, the service goes down, then the lies and fangs come out.

The Mean Girls are in charge, outright lying about the review of your policies. When questioned they get real nasty, threatening you with insurance inspections and cancellations.

No longer are they sharp and smart, but become ignorant and play stupid, missing the simplest of saving incentives.

To add insult to injury, they aren't even nice anymore. They are The Bully Little Mean Girls of the Baker Agency.

Mudflap, Completely Out !

The Law is the Law

(Lawyers)

Mudflap likes lawyers. They are mostly level-headed, practical, and generally all-around good people to do business with.

If you read the first book, you know he doesn't like Blood Sucking Divorce Lawyers.

The only time you want a lawyer is to close some kinda business arrangement or to do personal estate work.

Any other reason and you're not having fun.

There is this one lawyer who Mudflap knows personally, and he is thee deal maker of Hartford. A total big shot. He's the one to go to when you kill someone and want to get off.

Last time Mudflap worked for him, he shorted the check and said, "You're going to eat this for me."

His wife is a judge. She made her carpenter change out the whole cabinet system (for free) that he had installed in her kitchen because "she" didn't like the color "she" picked out. The poor guy was in tears as he was loading them into his truck.

Is that the proper conduct for a judge? Is that what you would call being fair?

He's the Big Shot and has been taking pieces of people his whole life, losing pieces of himself as an outcome.

Hold on to yourself, don't let pieces slip away.
Mudflap, Over and Out !

(Responsible Gun Ownership)

Guns are and will always be part of the United States of America.

Guns fight Bullies.
Bullies have Guns.

It's a not so, Merry-go-Round.

Mudflap is an NRA member and he is pro background checks, too.
Over and Out !

(The Economy)

Big George Bush and The Trickle-Down Economics

Nourishment from the Top, like the spring rains fall down.

All the wealthy people Mudflap ever knew had real estate that grew more valuable over time.

Mudflap believed, he invested, he got the deductions, they helped him hang on through the hard times. He toughed it out for decades but over thirty years later the payoff just was not there.

Tough it out some more, it's become regular business for the middle class.

MF. Out !

131

(Finance Educator)

There was a Finance Professor from U-Conn who lived on Beacon Hill, a high-end neighborhood Mudflap works in. But he didn't understand the simple economics of business and relationships. He didn't appreciate quality and only looked in his pockets instead of the world around him.

Mudflap's son went to U-Conn and majored in actuarial science. He took another major in finance too.

He told Mudflap the finance course was so simplistic that they were handing out degrees like lollipops.

Keep that in mind next time a financial advisor tries to sell you something.

MF. Tired of Money Bullies and Out !

The Queen of the Shakedown

She is all class,
charming everyone who encounters her.

The serfs fall to her feet,
thrilled to be of service.

The elite are thrilled in her presence,
as well.

She drifts through the finest dust,
and rolls in the thickest mud.

Always coming up with the longest stick,
and out of the muck with the gold watch.

She walks down a staircase so elegantly
that it appears she is floating like an apparition.

She will skin you alive with the sweetest smile,
and leave you begging for more.

Everyone loves to be taken advantage of by her.

She knows how to play.
She knows how to rule.

She is The Queen of the Shake Down.

She is Rachel.

MF. Fondly and Respectfully, Out !

133

Jay Alden Bailey

(Dr. Bully)

This could be a book but I will condense it for you and me.

Mudflap was told not to print this story. He was told that he can't print this story. But they never should have said, "Don't dare print that story."

Mudflap has worked in West Hartford for decades; it's a residential town with all sorts of white-collar professionals of every kind. His clients were like a list of the who's who of Hartford, many high-quality people at the top levels of their fields.

For the first 29 years of his career, his primary physicians were old retired doctors who were his buddies but, sadly, one by one they died, leaving Mudflap at 50 years old looking for a primary doctor.

The first legitimate physical Mudflap had in over 30 years was with his last client/doctor/friend. He is a top cardiologist and nutritionist. Mudflap was a big fan of his outlook on the way diet affects health care; commonly many doctors are lacking in the nutritional realm. (Check out the book *Dead Doctors Don't Lie*.)

Mudflap got a real physical and his cherry popped with his first digital exam. His friend was a bit squeamish and told him to double check the exam with a specialist. It was becoming too much for Mudflap already, right out of the starting gate, so he skipped a couple more years of checkups.

Mudflap's health care insurer wanted him to get regular exams, forcing him to find a doctor. So, he decided to get someone completely unrelated to his client base, not wanting to burden his friends anymore now that he had aging issues, and obviously he was going to start needing more regular care.

134

Mudflap does have a phobia of doctors and hospitals and when he confided that fact to a doctor friend he was told, "That's a healthy phobia to have, stay out of hospitals." Well, that didn't really help ease Mudflap's mind.

Mudflap wanted to choose someone young enough to see him through his aging process but old enough to be properly experienced.

He picked one of the big Hartford-area health care organizations and got into the system.

Years went by unremarkably. He had a doctor with a calm demeanor who gave him light physicals; one included a digital but Mudflap, uncomfortable with the process, started to count on blood work instead, having the doctor focus on his PSA test and other blood work information.

Then things started to go the wrong way.

Mudflap took care of himself all the past years, toughing out his injuries common to his physical activities. He confided in doctors only as a last resort.

Aging stinks and turning 60 years old most definitely changes your body, no matter how good of shape you're in.

First, Mudflap became aware of a hernia in his groin, a lump. Cancer is like the worst swear word, it makes people cringe at the thought. Mudflap figured out the lump was a hernia. Being aware of things, he didn't panic and thought it would go away.

Then not much later, he had a real scare. After an evening conjugal session with his wife, he was rubbing his testicles and realized there was some kinda of miscount. 1,2 and 3? 1,2 and 3? This isn't good thought Mudflap, I'm done, check out time.

135

He went around depressed for a few days, feeling really sorry for himself. Thinking about how to wrap up his estate quickly for his girls (wife and daughter) and what to do about unsettled scores.

Finally, he confided to his wife, to prepare her for the end; she quickly got on her phone and started looking up information. To Mudflap's great relief, this is what they found out.

If you have a lump on a testicle it's probably cancer. But if you clearly have an extra one floating around, it is most likely just a benign fatty cyst.

Well, that was a great relief and changed everything.

Mudflap wasn't worried about anything anymore, he planned to ignore both lumps. At the DOT driver's medical exam, the doctor asked to check him for a hernia and Mudflap said "Oh, yes. I do have one but I have had lots of injuries over the years and I have never been cut open. I want to let it heal itself."

The Doctor gave Mudflap a heads up and told him, "This isn't something that's just going to go away on its own. It's going to only get worst and you could end up with a bag on your side if you're not careful."

That woke Mudflap up. And the doctor was right. A few months later (late spring) the hernia was beginning to hurt.

So, Mudflap decided to wait till his fall-time regular physical and schedule his surgery for winter.

November came and physical went well as usual. Mudflap told the doctor about his experience with the other doctor at the DOT exam and the hernia, everything was going normally, no problems.

After the hernia was addressed, blood work and pre-op exam scheduled, Mudflap said, "Oh, by the way, I have something else I would like to tell you about."

(Here we go !)

Mudflap said, "I found something else but I'm not really worried about it. I thought you should know in case it gets worse." He told the doctor about how he had found the extra testicle and that he was sure it was clearly an independent cyst and had even become quite comfortable with it, stating, "Everybody knows I have more balls than brains." He also thought to himself that it's probably storing extra testosterone, helping him fight the aging process.

The usually calm doctor became very excited and said, "It could be cancer. I have to check it." Mudflap repeated that he knew what he had and was not worried but the doctor insisted on giving an exam saying, "I have to check."

Mudflap was taken aback by his hyper behavior and didn't want to argue. The doctor aggressively went at his testicles with way too much force. Mudflap told him, "Stop, you're hurting me." But the doctor did not pay attention to him. He was going at him like rabid rodent, ripping, tearing, and pulling his balls apart.

At the end of the exam, he calmed down and went to his computer. He brought up pictures of genitals and cysts, explaining to Mudflap exactly what he had already explained to the doctor.

Mudflap was sore and upset with the doctor but held his cool. Not wanting to make a fuss because getting his hernia fixed was more important, he knew causing trouble about the exam was not going to help him. He left the office feeling assaulted.

The next day he was feeling really sore, called the doctor's office and asked to speak with him.

Jay Alden Bailey

The lady informed Mudflap that the doctor was too busy for routine follow ups and she could help him. He explained the situation and that he was in a lot of pain. She replied with a cavalier attitude, "Just put your feet up for a few days and ice them." He didn't like her chuckle and said, "I have to work for a living. I don't have the time to sit around for three days with my feet up." She said, "Well, that's too bad, there is nothing we can do. It's normal to be hurting after exams, it will go away."

Three days later he called the office and asked to speak to the doctor again, remaining calm, not wanting to cause any commotion. He refused a nurse's assistance and, as politely as possible, asked for the doctor to return his call.

It was a week before Mudflap heard back from the doctor. Mudflap was still in pain all the time, and Doctor T, which we will call him for "Twit", was very short and dismissive. He said, "Take some ibuprofen."

Exactly one month later, Mudflap, still in regular pain, called Dr.T's office asking for a return call. He did not receive any reply at all.

Finally, the pre-op exam that was scheduled with the surgeon came and everything went well. Mudflap liked the surgeon, and he confided in him about his exam pain from Dr.T. He told him he was sorry that he had even told T. about the cyst at all.

His eyes widened at the story and said, "It shouldn't affect the surgery and I am glad you told me. Never keep anything from your doctor, especially your surgeon."

Another appointment was scheduled with T. for pre-op blood work, etc., and Mudflap asked him why he had not returned his call. Dr. T. replied, "I did not get the message, why didn't you call again?" Mudflap said, "I wasn't going to keep pestering you. I expected a call back." T. became very nasty and aggressive. Mudflap, taken aback, was not going to argue because he was afraid T. would somehow interfere with the upcoming surgery.

Mudflap, for the second time, left T.'s office feeling assaulted.

A week or so after the surgery, Mudflap was feeling pain more from T.s' exam than from the surgery itself. He confided in a doctor friend/client he had known for over 30 years, finding out from that conversation that the original advice to ice his groin was most likely not the best choice.

Mudflap, not being stupid and knowing his own body well, never did take that advice anyway.

Mudflap called T.'s office again and got the original lady on the phone who had given him the bad advice. Recognizing his name and voice, she grilled him for information. He was not interested in confiding anything more to her and asked to speak to the office manager.

With an attitude, she reluctantly connected Mudflap to the "Office Hawk" watching over everybody. She was very nice and listened carefully to Mudflap's complaint. He not only explained the exam injury itself, but T.'s no-call-back treatment and his nasty demeanor, as well as the staff's bad advice and humorous attitude, too.

As the conversation went on, Mudflap found out that the original advice given to him was not that of a nurse. Ms. Ice was only the receptionist. That really floored Mudflap, his health care was left in the hands of a giggling receptionist who was not qualified.

A complaint was formally filed and Mudflap was scheduled to talk with the commanding office doctor who was in charge of all the doctors and nurses.

Jay Alden Bailey

When Mudflap returned Ms. Hawk's call, the receptionist Ms. Ice was extremely belligerent to Mudflap when he gave his name. She said, "We know who you are!" And started to reprimand him for daring to complain and told him, "Because of you I may lose my job." Then she abruptly passed the call to the Hawk.

Well, the original chuckling, cavalier attitude of Ms. Ice was gone and she didn't think Mudflap's pain was as much of a joke as she originally thought. Mudflap, now on the offensive, chuckled to himself as he felt fear running through the herd. "We know who you are!"

What does "we" mean? Were Mudflap's health issues the topic of the entire office?

A week to ten days later, Mudflap was on his way to see the head doctor of the office for the follow-up on the complaints. Coincidently, he was listening to NPR which never has advertisements, and they were selling a personal injury lawyer.

The head doctor gave Mudflap a small window of time because she was so very busy. He was completely understanding about the value of her time and he was early and waiting.

This was not a consultation it was more of a "Stone-Wall." Mudflap got very little out of her and was quickly dismissed by Dr. Stone. She advised that there should be additional exams made. Mudflap said, "No, that's not happening. I have had enough injuries for the moment."

One interesting fact emerged from the meeting. Stone said she had asked T. why didn't he return Mudflap's last call and he replied to her, "I didn't call him back because I knew he was coming in for another exam for the hernia pre-op, and I was going to address him then."

"Well, that's interesting," Mudflap said. "Because he told me he didn't get the call at all and had asked me why I didn't keep trying?"

Point being, T. either lied to Mudflap or lied to Stone, but regardless, he was caught in a lie.

Mudflap had been in business for 40 years at this point and the two things he dislikes the most are #1 not returning calls. He will not do business with anyone who does not reply. And #2 is lying. He totally dislikes liars and once caught, questions everything thereafter that comes out of their mouth.

And his doctor? Is he completely out of touch? It's immoral behavior for a doctor to lie his way out of a problem, like some bad child who's been caught doing something.

Mudflap has experienced many times the lowest people in his life whose first instinct, when confronted with bad behavior of any kind, is to lie their way out. He detests such actions and from his doctor? He found it completely absurd. The lower IQ person immediately turns to a lie, whereas the higher IQ person will fess up to a bad decision and/or try to correct their mistake.

Dr. Stonewall tried her best, doing her job to stop all forward actions. Mudflap called the injury lawyer who advertised on NPR and found out some interesting information. There is no venue for medical claims under $250,000 and was advised to contact him again when he felt the claim had reached that level.

Mudflap now was really mad at the lying doctor who hurt him and went back to the Hawk, going through Ms. Ice again who now finally learned to shut her mouth, and just connected Mudflap.

He tried to make a small claim through the inter-workings on the company's system and was confronted by their staff member who at first seemed receptive and then pushed forward more lies and cover-up. The Hawk was the only person who seemed to care at all and was frustrated herself at not receiving replies and getting stonewalled, too.

Mudflap wrote to the president of the large Hartford-area health care organization and was headed off by the last line of defense. Ms. Begging-Your-Forgiveness, who, like the claims personnel, at first seemed concerned and then quickly became mean. She wrote a carefully crafted letter of shallow, insincere apologies.

Ms. Beggingly shut the door with more bullying twisted truths and cover-up.

In the end, it does not matter if they hurt you or disregard your privacy and you become the office joke. They can treat you any way they want and do whatever they please. Bully for them!

Mudflap wrote one last letter to the president of the organization, pretty sure the letters never really reached his desk anyway, but his last statement was, "Are you going to do anything about the staff's behavior or are you the President of Hartford Don't Care?"

Mudflap, of course, never heard back from anyone. And still, after a long hard day at work, and sometimes in the morning as he wakes up, he still feels his hernia area as well as his exam injury.

Later he told the story to an old client he had who was still in service, 35 years of loyalty. After hearing the whole thing, this warm, liberal lady gave an unsupportive, cold reply, **"Welcome to the world of women, it happens to us all the time."**

Mudflap, Over and Out !

P.S. Real Time: Mudflap was outdone in the dark humor department by one of his doctor buddies. With the virus in full swing, Mudflap no longer goes out to the coffee shop, eliminating the relaxing, mid-morning ritual break.

After he drank the coffee his friend made him, Dr. Rah ha-ha-hul told him, "I think I had the virus. My wife and I have had some mild symptoms but we are ok now." Mudflap said, "Gee, thanks for telling me after I drank the coffee." He smiled and said, "Wash your hands, you will be fine."

Good one, Doc. !
MF. Out !

143

Jay Alden Bailey

(Aging)

Finally, as you age beyond your capabilities, you lose your liberties.

Don't go complacently, kick and scream all the way.

Mudflap, Over and Out !

There was an old doctor buddy of Mudflap's going like a gang buster into his nineties. He was active and driving around, acting like a young guy, full of life, he was a hell of a man. We will call him Dr. Man.

But there came a time when his wife no longer wanted to keep up with the house and property. She decided to seek a retirement community, with a future for assisted living included in the retirement residential package.

The idea was to make everything easier and more secure for their futures. Dr. Man went along with the whole thing, but he did start to have reservations about the loss of privacy and some freedoms. The wife was a common-sense lady, stood her ground and pointed out all the sensible reasons behind their decision to make the big move.

As the last tree and landscape service wrapped up with the doctor, he talked to Mudflap about all the amenities at the new residence. He was going on about the convenient parking and vehicle-related issues. He was trying to stay up beat as he talked about it all, but it was obvious that he really was trying to sell it more to himself; his biggest question was mostly about his freedom.

144

Mudflap said goodbye to his friend and his last bit of advice was, "First it's the house, next it will be your car. Better watch out. Hold on tight to your keys, Man."

MF. Out !

P.S. Real Time:
Coincidently, Mudflap ran into Dr. Man the very next day after writing about him. It had been many years, at least six, seven, or more. The good doctor was walking in the arms of his wife, both keeping the other steady. Everyone was smiles. Mudflap gave them both a hug and told Man about the book and that he was in it. Turns out, just in the past couple of months, his doctor convinced him to stop driving because he was being harassed constantly by Man's children. After he pleaded his case again and again, Dr. Man finally agreed to give up driving at 99 years young. Mudflap thought he looked great and told him, "If anybody is making it past 110 years, it is going to be you." Keep up the pace Man!

MF.> Out !

(Prejudice)

Now, here is a subject that at first seems a common issue to address, but when it turns into a discussion, it becomes taboo. No matter what you say about racism, somebody is going to have a problem with it.

Women are still treated horribly in many venues. Now, the #MeToo movement can sometimes go too far; but that's the consequence of all the negative actions that have come before.

Mudflap started to address prejudice in his first book. Experiencing it as a young man from Connecticut, working in Virginia, he was labeled "Yankee Boy." And again, as a young contractor working in Maine, he was called "The Flatlander."

Mudflap's point was supposed to be taken from a "White Male's" confused point of view; we are not a minority. Are we not at the top of the food chain? It seems easy for white males to look down their noses at everybody else and it's a bit of a shock when the situation is reversed.

Aww, too bad for the poor disenfranchised white males around the nation who feel their country is being taken away from them. They still quickly and conveniently forget and disregard the genocide of the Native Americans. Also, the enslavement and mass importation of another whole race from Africa.

Did you know, at the Nuremberg trials, the Nazis were in shock at the hypocrisy of the Americans? And that was part of their defense. But they were quickly squashed down with the "Librarian Scowl" and many were imprisoned for life or executed.

What legacy will the white race leave behind in 100 years and more into the future? As the melting pot that is America continues to grow and more ingredients are added, will the self-evident truths be admired by everyone? Will they all say, "Yes, George Washington and the rest of them knew that all men and women are created equal." Will the world and all its races look up to the White Englishmen as visionaries? Or will they see them as hypocrites? That view of the white race in the future depends on how we carry the policy of equality forward.

Again, in the first book, Mudflap tried to simply point out that Black Americans still don't get the respect they not only deserve but have earned. Whenever he tries to speak up about the issue, he is combated by resistance and he has been told not to put it in his book.

It's always about precedent, so that's why Mudflap uses the Native Americans and African-Americans as the best examples. They have been persecuted for the longest time and at the most severe levels. And both different races have fought on our side during all the wars from the very beginning.

People say things like, "You will sound condescending." Another thing they go on about is in statements like, "they don't want your help," and "they don't need help. They get too much help already, that's the problem."

The problem with prejudice is, it is just like bullies, it will be and they will always be here. The way Mudflap sees it, the ammunition in the fight comes down to one simple word "respect."

The sooner we all get that from everybody on both sides of politics, races and genders, everybody in the entire spectrum, and that includes all life and the planet as a whole, the sooner 90% of our problems will be over.

Many would debate that's an over simplification; true, because another word that comes into play, too, is "resistance."

Embrace the changing world, stop resistance, show respect to everyone and everything.

That's fighting prejudice.
Mudflap, Over and Out !

P.S. Real Time: It's a panic! The Coronavirus threatens to cross borders. New Yorkers have been dubbed "The Walking Dead." Vehicles with NY plates are being stopped, harassed and turned back. New Yorkers are now considered "Zombies."

P.P.S. Real Time: Another African-American citizen killed by the police. Protests rise up all over the nation. Trump threatens retaliation with the Army. Wouldn't it be better if he called out for the policemen's heads? Would a show of support not defuse the situation rather than make it worse? The story is still unfolding.

P.P.P.S. Real Time: Again, another incident during the first week of protest. /// The Wendy's drive-through killing. He dared to resist arrest and now he's dead.

Oh, yeah, how about the guy a few years back choked to death for selling single cigarettes. And the video of the guy being shot in the back as he ran away. Wait, which video?

MF. ? ? ?

Scary Harry

Mudflap has a friend who is a contractor too. He has all sorts of stories of wild escapades and ball crunching humor.

I will sum up his twisted sense of fun with one of his favorite tales.

There was this kitchen range left out in front of someone's yard by the roadside with a sign on it that said, "Free."

Scary stopped and checked it out. It was in great condition and he had the perfect home for it. So, he loaded it up, installed it right way, and was very happy with the outcome.

Two years later it burnt out and stopped working. Scary loaded it up in his truck and in the middle of the night he brought it back to the spot in the front yard where he had acquired it.

When the people woke up, their range was back from two years ago with a sign on it that read "Thanks."

Imagine what he would do to you if you crossed him.

The moral of the story:
Next time you have an issue with a contractor, and you contemplate shortchanging them, or dare to mess with their schedule, etc., think about Scary Harry and how would he react?

MF.> Out !

Jay Alden Bailey

Scary Harry has a friend named Joe. The story goes like this:

(Joe, his Daughter and the Boys)

A common story throughout history, repeating like the generations themselves.

Some things never change.
Mudflap, Over and Out !

Joe's daughter kept boyfriends like puppy dogs. He was never worried about them taking advantage of her because she was always clearly in charge.

She would lead her boys around like they were on a leash. Often, they were just tagging at her heels.

Once, Joe observed one of the boy's uneasiness. Realizing the boy did not know what to do with himself, Joe gave the boy some advice. He said, "You are here at the pleasure of the Princess. I suggest that you do not bore her." "Right," the boy said and popped up and started paying more attention.

Later that day, Joe was working in his yard and asked for a hand in his shipping container. The boy hesitated and didn't want to step inside with him. Seeing the nervous expression on the poor kid's face made Joe laugh, and he couldn't resist taunting the anxious one and said to him, "This isn't the container you have to worry about, it's the one buried underneath that should bother you." The boy jumped back and exclaimed, "You got one underneath here?" Straight-faced Joe replied, "Yes, come here and take a look." The kid froze and looked as though he was going to pee his pants until

150

Joe starting laughing out loud saying, "Don't be such a pussy." That seemed to break the ice and for the rest of the day the boy was very helpful every chance he got.

Then the next two boys in line were real players, lazy with attitude issues.

Joe calls his daughter's house "Princess Airport," because there is always some pilot circling and requesting permission to land. There is always one in the hanger. There is always one on the runway getting the instructions for take-off. And there is always another one in the air going on to another location.

The next one Joe had to deal with was Free Boy. After a while, when he never seemed to go home and was there all the time, Joe suggested he start to pay rent or start going home once in a while. The master of the free load said, "Gee, I would really like to help you out, paying your bills and all, but I have my money tied up in investments."

Princess needed some space and Free Boy wanted drama as he departed for an adventure. He was going off to the Swiss Alps, to live at an old-world farm and learn the ancient ways of making cheese. Such a grand dream, all the while living off his parents and Joe, too.

He was hanging around all the time, even had a free truck his father gave him to use, and he couldn't even take out his trash. He left for his trek and when Joe came to help his daughter clean up, he found, literally, piles of garbage in bags stuffed everywhere. He had recyclables stacked high behind the back door, forehead height. There was filthy rotting kitchen garbage hiding in-between the bags of cleaner garbage.

Free Boy left the mudroom full of his clothes, assorted junk, and exactly one dozen pairs of shoes. These were not stacked neatly in a row, but tossed everywhere, stuffed between all the piles of crap in everything you could imagine. One pair was brand new, still had the tags on them, stained and in separate places.

Who in their right mind would leave someone else to clean up their mess like that? Especially after you have been helped out.

He was going off for his tour and expected everyone to trip over his belongings for three months? Was this guy for real?

Joe was boiling mad at the Cheezee Free Boy who had left such a God-awful mess for everyone else.

Then two weeks later he came back because the farm was not accepting new recruits at that current time. He blew all that air-fare and travel money without doing his homework?

And next he wanted to move right back in with daughter? Yeah, right! She threw Joe quickly under the bus, telling Cheezee Boy, "Sorry, my dad says you can't move back, clean out the rest of your stuff." Aww, poor Cheezee. He cried what a pain in the ass it was to gather up the other belongings he had left all over the house. He bitched and moaned the whole day as he cleaned up the rest of his mess. What a spoiled brat.

A year later Cheezee called to ask for more of his things that he had forgotten. He called multiple times for this item and that. Last time Joe heard he was still griping about something he left.

What father can relate to anyone so spoiled, lazy, and completely insensitive to everyone around them? This is the product of the "New Millenniums' Over-Protective Parents." They have spawned the worst bunch of babies ever to grace the planet.

He flew across to the Alps and back. Then went to the West Coast and back again. He couldn't figure out why everyone was not waiting with open arms ready to keep cleaning up after him, again.

Last Joe heard, Cheezee was looking for some vinyl records he had left. He's still bothering The Princess, not understanding that he has a one-way flight schedule, with no plan for a return-route. While Cheezee was still looking for lost luggage, the next Bum who landed at the airport was already receiving departing instructions.

He landed, all feathers fluttering in the air and elbows swinging, leaving Cheezee no room for a request to land. Joe made it very clear that he didn't want to be cleaning up after another one of the Princess's boyfriends; all he wanted from the new one was minimum aggravation.

Instead he got the Minimum Effort Guy. He was a trainer not a keeper. The Princess found out the hard way, you can't help people who won't help themselves.

When Minimum landed, he at first seemed self-sufficient: a certified tradesman with a job. But soon his living situation was being disrupted and he needed help.

The Princess wanted Joe to give Minimum a break because he was in a squeeze. Joe, who was still sore from Cheezee, said, "Mini is not my problem." The Princess replied, "If I am going to be with Mini, and he needs help, and he is costing me, then it's costing you. So, Mini is your problem."

How's that one? As off the wall as it is, sadly, she was right. Mini was Joe's problem.

So Mini got helped and he started making a mess right away. The garbage thing started, too; the bags were piling up again. Joe put the brakes on it fast, not using innuendos. He spoke a clean, clear message: he didn't want his property trashed.

Joe always asks things nicely on the first request. The second request he is still polite, but the reminder has a slight tone to it. At the third request there is irritation in that tone. The fourth time Joe has to ask for something, he starts a reprimand and it just goes downhill real fast after that.

When Joe was getting sick of the mess and the deja vu moment of Cheezee Boy, he asked Mini the Man Boy to get up to speed and start taking proper care of the place.

Then, the little boy who was being helped had the nerve to try a bully tactic on Joe. He said, "Do you want us to move out?" Oh, really? If Joe didn't want to put up with Mini's mess and garbage, the little bully was going to take is daughter and go? Where?

Without a security deposit they would have to move in on someone else. But that's regular business for a bum like Mini the Man Boy. Just share the next space and clutter up someone's life until you get thrown out again. Around and around he goes and now he's going take the Princess with him to live the life of a parasite?

All these Man-Boys have the same M.O. They want cheap, or free, living expenses and always want use of the Princess's vehicle, too. Mini Boy's car was sitting so long the tires were sinking into the ground.

Finally, he got his flight request served to him for the exact same reason Cheezee got his. The Princess got sick of waiting on him as he sat around wallowing deeper and deeper in his mess; the same crappy scene played out like a carbon copy.

Mini the Man Boy's flight took off on the Princess's time schedule. She allowed more return flights for cargo planes only; no passengers were allowed to step on to the tarmac.

Mini went to live with his poor unsuspecting aunt, who was the last person in his family willing to put up with him. It just may be the perfect relationship because he can live for free, and she is blind and won't see the messes the boy makes. Joe does wonder how it will go when she starts to trip over the piles of crap. I'll bet ya, she starts to complain. Even a blind person can see a loser like Mini the Man Boy.

"This is Air Traffic Control. Flight 101 from Brooklyn now given clearance to land on the primary runway. Passenger required to lock down his seat belt, prepare for turbulence and a fast landing. Be careful not to fall on your exit from the plane, and expect slippery conditions on the tarmac.

Please be advised: there are no insurance claim venues available, enter the premises at your own risk. Keep a parachute handy at all times on subsequent shuttle flights to and from the Jet Port.

Ejection can occur at a moment's notice and at any altitude per the whims and pleasure of the Princess. Keep your baggage under control and do not wait for the flight attendant to be of service or to clean up after you. Help yourself at every possible juncture you encounter. Don't get too comfortable and start expecting too many services. Be polite at all times and maintain the highest respect for the Princess. Avoid the Security Force. They have been known to cause trouble and delay you. Don't get in the way of the Maintenance Crew or disrupt their routines, it can create a serious backlash. Assume nothing except a demand for a quick departure for poor and/or substandard behavior.

Air Traffic Control, Over and Out !"

Good luck, Flight 101. You're going to need a strong "Will" to survive. Joe hopes there is a real Man on board; the Service Team is tired of baby-sitting.

We all are here serving at the pleasure of the Princesses. I suggest no one bore them.

Or Risk the Pike.

**Good Luck, Joe, you're going to need it.
Mudflap,Over and Out !**

(The Sweetie)

There was this really nice, sweet lady who was on a vacation in Rio with a new boyfriend when the Coronavirus struck. They finished their trip at first not in a panic, as there were no cases in the area. But as they checked the flights at the airport, tensions were escalating. The Sweetie wanted to catch the next plane out, becoming anxious to get home. Her Boy Friend was not ready to leave; he wanted to stay another night and catch their scheduled flight.

The Sweetie wanted out. Boy didn't get the memo: "Pay attention to the desires of the Sweetie, do not balk!" She was frustrated at his cavalier attitude and her anxiety spiked. His concern to save a couple of bucks over the wishes of the Sweetie shook her confidence.

He refused to help her as she struggled with the smart phone and the Internet. They missed the flight available and stayed the night in a hotel, maintaining the Boy's schedule.

The next 24 hours was like putting the Sweetie in a pressure cooker; her anxiety just kept growing.

They made it back to the States and sequestered themselves at Sweetie's house for the 12 days that followed. The Sweetie never got over the shock and anxiety of being trapped in a place she didn't want to be in by a Man Boy who couldn't make a proper decision.

Any good husband will tell you, when a woman wants out of a place and has high anxiety over a situation, you have to act and take care of her wishes, period.

It's not the time to balk or be worried about saving a few bucks. A real man knows how to handle a woman, and sometimes that means giving in and setting your own wishes and/or agendas aside.

You can't always get what you want. But all the time you're going to get what you deserve.

The Sweetie never got over the bad choice. Boy failed to make the right calculations and maneuver properly.

After 12 more days stuck sequestered with him, he got his flight notice and was sent out into the plague. Back to the high-risk zone to face it on his own.

The Sweetie needed time alone to recuperate and recharge with her puppy.

Don't cross a Sweetie.
MF.> Out !

**Don't get too comfortable
and make others uncomfortable.
MF.**

Familiarity Breeds Contempt

The old Aesop thing again: Mudflap has the exact same problem with different people in every situation -- business and personal.

He clearly defines his position or a request, stating exactly what he wants and/or expects to give. Then afterwards, the people get too comfortable, decide to change their expectations, and force that change onto Mudflap.

I think a lot of people can relate to that situation.

The true level determining the quality of any individual is the strength they show when backing up their word with their actions.

Abuse of a trust, or trying to change an outcome to gain anything by taking advantage of someone's good nature, is not only a form of bullying, it is immoral.

It's a topic that could go on for hours, but I think that sums it up.

**Abusers, watch out for that sharp razor edge of Karma!
Mudflap, Over and Out !**

Jay Alden Bailey

(Bullies play dress up.)

The old saying "Dress for success," has a simple message: Clean up your act, look sharp, and show some discipline. It has many social nuances, too, and can have a bullying twist to it.

In schools, kids can be ostracized for modest clothing. Cliques can be cruel in high-end towns where parents can afford to dress their children in designer outfits. That's why private schools have uniforms, so as not to distract students with this social issue, and the uniforms show that degree of discipline, too.

You have to dress for what you want to be: If you want to hang out at the biker bar, get some tattoos and put on leather, or you will get bullied by walking in with your polo shirt. In reverse, don't expect to be ingratiated at the golf club in your biker jacket with your nose pierced.

We are liberal and conservative. Everybody has their rights. That's what makes us a great nation. We let extreme people be who they are. Even though we fought the second World War to defeat the fascists, we still allow the Nazi party to exist in America today.

They may be scary people, but the reality is they will not take us over. Little old ladies would beat them with brooms if they tried to overthrow America. They are just scared bullies. A bunch of little white boys playing dress up, parading around, and trying to look tough.

Mudflap's son became a "Budding Actuary" and got a job at a good insurance company. From the beginning Mudflap wanted his son to focus on getting a management position. So, he guided his math-minded boy, suggesting he take finance as a second major, so he could not only crunch the numbers but could apply them.

Mudflap The Gloves Come Off

He wanted his boy to look sharp as he entered the working world and got him proper clothes, a selection of suits and ties. Mudflap, himself, as a tree cutter, destroys his clothes and is comfortable in worn, often shredded attire. He looks like he just crawled out from under a stump because he probably just did.

Mudflap preached to his son that his clothes are like his tools and how important looking good at the office is for his future. He was very disappointed to hear that the whole office, bosses and interns alike, were dressed down in a very casual style.

But the boy took the idea of being well-dressed seriously and, despite the casual dress of the entire office, he continued to wear his tie every day.

Mudflap, always seeing his son as a top executive, told him, "Subliminally you are telling everyone that you are a boss, a top manager, and you take your job and your position seriously. Keep dressing well, and I'm glad you like your tie, keep wearing it."

Mr. Math finally passed his last level of actuarial exams, and his superiors are talking to him about a management position. Working hard and showing some discipline does seem to get you the attention you deserve.

So, straighten your tie and look the part you want to play. Dress in rags or in drag. Become what you want to be and what makes you feel good, just don't be a bully and push it on others.

Mudflap, Over and Out !

Footwear:

Shoes Make the Man

Women are more stylish, and it's harder to read their personalities through footwear, but not impossible; they too, fall into stereotypes. If you want to read a man, start paying attention to what the guy has on his feet; shoes clearly send a message. Bosses and the higher-ranking wear expensive, stylish shoes, even at home. Wealthy people enjoy expensive footwear, too. Sneakers are the universal show of comfort and activity, a most sensible form of foot attire.

Mudflap likes sneakers, but hates the debris they collect inside, especially from walking on gravel roads or in the woods. His first and most often selected foot gear is the work boot. It does it all, from support and comfort for getting the job done, to hiking and just banging around. Nothing compares to having boots on your feet.

Who do you want on your side in a bar fight, the guy with sneakers, or the one in boots?

Many carpenters and other tradesmen wear sneakers on the job. They are easy to slip on and off and are cool in summer, enabling you to bounce around and get a lot of work done comfortably.

Athletes and the active live in sneakers, as well as people who suffer from foot pain.

When Mudflap was a little boy, he thought it was funny when he saw a sign in a shop window with a big foot and bold print saying, "The Foot Doctor."

Mudflap doesn't run to doctors crying about his aches and pains, but he has found as he has aged that his Podiatrist is his most important doctor of them all. If your feet aren't right than neither is your whole body, from ankles to knees, back and hips, all the way to your shoulders and neck. All are affected by your feet. He no longer laughs and takes "The Foot Doctor" seriously.

A man in sandals isn't getting a lot of physical work done, and the flip-flop is the lowest form of footgear when it comes to getting chores or any real work accomplished.

Many women love flip-flops, and Mudflap's wife and daughter are in them all the time. But he feels that men in flip-flops aren't really taking the day seriously: they scream idleness, relaxation, and laziness.

Footwear could be a book on its own.

The next time you're sizing up someone take a look at their feet. It will tell you a lot about the person and their expectations of the day ahead.

Mudflap, Boots laced tight, and Out !

****

Mudflap is Done with Bullies and Pests.

On the Road of Life

Just when life takes a turn and you think you know where it is leading you, Wham, you run into a sharp curve and off you go in another direction.

Where you think you're going is not always where you are supposed to be. The greater forces around us lead and/or obstruct us, guiding everyone along to their proper paths.

The key is to recognize the terrain you have to cross, before you get in too deep and realize there were better paths you could have taken.

The guides in the road may adjust your thinking; even though you were steadfast on one path, ideas and enlightenment may point you in a different direction.

An Old Proverb: "It's a Woman's Prerogative to Change Her Mind."

It's the time of "Women" and they are more in the forefront than ever.

Equality is in !
Get on board, Guys.
It's your Prerogative to Change your Minds, too.

Mudflap, Over and Out !

CHAPTER 4

Hurray for Us

Some people forget were they came from, maybe out of shame.

But too often, out of greed.

The feeling is you don't have to be nice to people on your way up, if you don't plan to ever go back down.

Careful, the top of the ladder is a tipsy place.

Mudflap, Over and Out !

Mudflap knows a local contractor who is now making it big with a patent on a particular set of tools for his particular trade. Now that he is making some real money, not just paddling around trying to make ends meet, he is becoming increasingly conservative and greedy.

He cries about paying health insurance costs and taxes to the state, but the reality is he is making so much more than anybody else his liabilities are different from the rest of us poor shmucks.

Too bad for the King of the Raggies. He is so rich, and the money is coming in so fast, he has to pay taxes.

Oh, my! Poor, poor, little King Raggie. He doesn't want any social services at all. He cries about giving his money away to the Evil State. He complains that they are coming to get him and pass his wealth out to all the homeless and the lazy.

And His wife, Queen of the Raggies, is a therapist getting money for patients through the State's social services. Money to pay for the type of services her King hates so much.

Times are tough, and she doesn't like her services being cut by the government. She wants the therapy sessions to go on for years; her patients never getting well, while she drains the system indefinitely.

She cries how her services are not being financed by the State in one breath and complains about the cost of her health care in the next. Citing their health care high costs are directly related to the fact that the lower income people, and state programs for the less fortunate, are being subsidized by their high premiums.

Unbelievable how she wants it both ways.

They both spit one big load of crap, thinking only of themselves.

He is such a big shot, so wealthy that he goes on all sorts of trips, but if you happen to call him when he is out of the country, he gets mad at you for increasing his phone bill.

"Waa, Waa!" Call a Waambulance! The King is having a crying attack.

If you're going to be a big shot and waste more money on fun than most people's food budget, don't whine.

Mudflap hates to hear "Fat Cats" whining, it's very unbecoming of their status.

Mudflap doesn't leave the country on a "Ha-Ha." He thinks flying around is a waste of the planet's resources.

They both are hard right, heavy-handed conservatives.

King Raggie is kind to no one, and he knows everybody's job better than they do. He is an immigrant from Canada who only became a citizen to vote against Obama, who he believed was going to give all our country's fortunes to the begging masses.

Queen Raggie is the hardline Catholic-type with no real compassion. She just gives lip service and keeps one hand out as she stuffs the money in her pocket with the other.

They talk about leaving Connecticut now that they have some money to hide. It wouldn't occur to them that people running with their money once that they have made it is part of why Connecticut has troubles.

They all want to go to Florida, the land of no taxes, live there for six months and a day and come back.

They talk the talk of anti-social services instead of becoming leaders in their community and doing something good for someone else. What kind of King and Queen is that? The kind that get dragged to the guillotine says Mudflap.

Mudflap is the story of many, as you know.

King Raggie is the story of many, too. He and his Queen are perfect examples of the uncompassionate, hardline extremists who care about only themselves.

True conservatives should be fiscally conscious but socially responsible.

That's what makes a strong community.

Mudflap, Over and Out !

CHAPTER 5

Mixed Company

Oil and Water.
Conservatives and Liberals.

Don't bring your left or right side to a party,
or it won't be a party at all.

Mudflap, Over and Out !

Mudflap used to be friends with the King of the Raggies until he turned to the Dark Side. Work was their common denominator; as contractors they shared a lot of similar experiences.

Even though the King did not need a free ticket to anything, Mudflap would get a kick out of paying his way at events. When Mudflap took his son shooting, he would invite the King along, too, never asking for ammunition money. Mudflap would pay homage to the King by picking up lunches and even movie tickets. Mudflap thought it was funny paying for such a big shot.

Then things went wrong when Mudflap and Wife went to a movie with the King and Queen.

"Oh, my!" "The Obama Movie", not the best venue for Liberal Wife and Right-Wing Queen.

The anti-entitlements attitude of the Queen, combined with her not liking her own entitlements cut for the Queen's Therapy Sessions, was a huge sticking point for Liberal Wife.

Around and around you go, back to the same place. Don't argue with a liberal. Just shake your head like you understand.

That was it for the social fun with the King and Queen. The friendship continued for a while but not with Wife involved.

Then Mudflap had safety issues that needed addressing associated with the King's work on Mudflap's house. It was not a big money maker for the King, just a nuisance His Richness didn't have time to bother with.

It did not matter how many times Mudflap had hired the King or paid for events; the King was becoming too important to have friends in as low places as Mudflap's.

He doesn't have time to address safety problems he made on properties; word of mouth referrals he no longer needs. His company now has a steady ad going on the radio, pulling in new business. (The most politically conservative station.) He needs new business all the time because he is quick to trash his old clients who he feels aren't worth his time anymore.

So, the King gets his place in the "spotlight" of what happens when a conservative right-wing guy makes it big!

And don't forget to leave your politics at home when going out in mixed company.

Mudflap, Over and Out !

P.S. Real Time: Mudflap knows another contractor who works for The King and Queen. He told Mudflap they are sequestered in their home, hiding from the "Coronavirus." The King opens the door to no one, not even his help. He does all his business through the glass, his phone, and the Internet. He and the Queen hide with their money, hoping to survive as the masses die out. They are the "Let them eat cake" kinda monarchs; the kind of rulers who disregard the needs of the people and are fearful of them, too.

Hide little King and Queen Raggie, hide from the plague and the guillotine.

MF> Out !

FISCALLY CONSCIOUS AND SOCIALLY RESPONSIBLE

That's the Moderate way to go politically.

Let the parties agree on this one philosophy and we will have progress.

M F> Out !

CHAPTER 6

CHURCH AND STATE

Religion in Politics

You cannot mix Church and State.

You cannot separate Church and State is more

like it.

Mudflap, Over and Out !

Churches are all around the centers of our towns. As towns were settled, the first place built to congregate was the church, not a town hall; more likely a tavern would be the first meeting place for politics. But once the church was built, it gave more than law to a settlement, it gave everyone a moral compass to guide them.

They are not only the center for the spiritual well-being of the people but the center of the community's social structure as a whole. A settlement with a church became a town that cared about its inhabitants, at least in theory it should. A question I'm sure the condemned witches in the original colonies would debate. Nothing like good old Puritan-style values to set the community straight.

Just like today when the government likes to scare us, and laws like the Patriot Act are put in place to protect us, original settlers had their share of fears and rules of law to protect them, too. The original Church and State working together, protecting the people from the evils of the world. The more things change, the more they remain the same.

Regardless of your personal view of an afterlife, the church's bigger influence on the mental and physical health good morals provide has a most undeniably positive effect on our society; so, for that reason, religion is a very good thing.

The Church is run by people (who else?) and people all have flaws, that's where the problems start. Religion has power, so does politics. Power corrupts, absolute power corrupts absolutely and spiraling down we go.

Religion, like politics, needs leaders, and leaders need to be held to a higher standard than the rest of the common people. That's why they are leaders; they are supposed to be better. What the common person expects from their leader is simply more than the average, better than the rest. If we don't get more and/or better, we experience real disappointment. The kind of disappointment that angers us, causes chaos and unrest in our society.

Mudflap, as a little child, with his brother and mom were outcasts of the church and the strict Irish-Catholic family.

Mudflap's mom, before she was married, was a telephone representative, during and after the war years, successful in her own right. She was very generous to the church. As a married woman with a successful husband, she had given even more.

When her husband cleaned out the family assets and left her broke with two young boys, she asked the church for a short-term loan, not a gift.

The priest's reply was, "What did you do to drive you husband away?" And, "We don't help people who sin like you!" The elder cousins felt the same way.

Mudflap and family were banished to another town to hide their shame. As a fallen woman, the mom could no longer accept communion. But despite her treatment, she brought the boys to church and said to them it was not the church itself who turned them away, it was the men in charge.

Mudflap was given a quarter to put in the basket every Sunday. Mudflap went shopping with his mom and her hand-clicker counter; he was all too aware of the limits of the grocery budget.

Cigarettes were 30 cents a pack and candy could be bought two for a penny, a quarter was a lot of candy. It was a real shake down for a little kid to give up more treats than he got all week long in one shot to a group who had cast them aside and made the mom cry.

Then as Mudflap got older a new priest took over. As a young adolescent Mudflap experienced a creepy leer from the priest and told his mom that he really didn't like the man. His mom said, "Don't be ridiculous he would never harm you."

As an adult years later in New Hartford, Mudflap watched the news and weather, regular morning business. There was a quick segment on the priest from Durham who was arrested for child abuse. Mudflap shook his head and said to his Wife, "I told everybody to watch out for that guy 29 yrs. ago."

Another story about Mudflap's mom:

175

When Mudflap was very young, a new style of entertainment evolved. When they lived alone in the rental between the highways, visitors started stopping to solicit their services. They were selling salvation, coming to them in an attempt to save their souls from eternal damnation.

They were the Jehovah's Witnesses. A pair first approached the house and the mom gave them the courtesy of listening for a few moments then she politely thanked them for their time and sent them away.

But they came back and pushed their sales on her again. The second time she was not as nice as she was before, telling them she had her faith and didn't need their help.

They had a message to give but weren't getting the message.

The third time they stopped she went off like a rocket. Man, could that lady scream! She scolded them terribly for not respecting her faith and her privacy.

The house became a target and a group of them stopped. This time the brother and Mudflap were aware of them and sounded the alarm. The boys yelled out, "They are back and there's more of them."

The kids hid in the background and watched the Mom in action as she faced the assault head on. Wow, could she go! How dare they intimidate and bully her and her boys!

This went on for a while, the group clearly determined to save the children from this Wicked Witch of Hell.

To this day, Mudflap always thinks of his mom when he sees a group of Witnesses combing the streets. They stopped at Mudflap's house when the Gulf War started back in the early 90's. If you're old enough to remember: Big George Bush had to push Saddam Husain out of Kuwait. (He knew better than to go in, try to occupy and destabilize a country like Iraq.) Anyway, the Jehovah's were really happy with the war. They were thrilled to inform Mudflap that it was the end of days and now it was his chance to be saved from the horrors of hell that his mom had condemned him to all those years ago. They looked at him in complete disbelief when he informed them that his soul was in good shape and he didn't need saving.

Even though the mom had been shunned by the Catholic priests because the father had left them, she never let it shake her faith.

The priests were bullies, the Jehovah's were bullies, too.

That didn't matter to the mom, she had a personal relationship with God. She understood that you don't need another person to be a conduit to God for you.

The church's place is to nurture one's soul and create a community bond with morals and behavior that should not only spread compassion throughout all of society, but should fight and, may I say, condemn the common bully.

Mudflap, as an adult, does not attend a church.

Mudflap did send his children to a Protestant church pre-school, and they got a lot out of it. Wife even did a little volunteer work for the church. Wife was brought up as a Quaker and had never been baptized.

Even though Mudflap at that point in his life was really disconnected from the church, he did appreciate what the little town's social circles did do through the different institutions. There are many Christian churches in the little town of New Hartford, all doing good things for the community.

The pastor did baptize the Wife and Mudflap's two children, all at once, in a little ceremony. Mudflap has to admit he really got a kick out of it, and it did make him feel good despite any questions he had about the true value of the process and his Fallen-Catholic status.

One of Mudflap's favorite clients (a college professor) prefers to be considered "a Recovering Catholic."

Mudflap liked that Wife took the kids to church and he went a few times, too. They did lose her, though, when a new vicar came and started preaching anti-women rhetoric. That particular church's denomination likes to keep their women in line. Didn't go over big with Sweet Little Wife, she is an independent thinker.

When the pastor questioned Mudflap about his religious orientation and found out he was raised Catholic, he indicated his particular church's proximity as to how close they were to the Catholics. He was taken aback when Mudflap's reply was, "You know, I have always noticed that all Protestants gauge themselves by how close or far away they are from the Catholics." His eyes widened as Mudflap went on, "Well, I'm there, I'm already Catholic."

I think fallen and or recovering Catholics have a hard time letting go of their faith. Like Mudflap's mom, they most likely have issues with the policies of the men running the church more than the actual religion itself. The faith a person grows up with, like the music they grow up with, has a lasting influence on their lives. You don't just change your taste in music, and you don't just change your faith in a cavalier manner either. Most likely, Catholics, drifting away to find another denomination, choose a particular church more out of community than in a change of belief.

The religion you grow up with is like your home; you always say where you grew up, like your hometown, that never changes. For that reason, I think it's hard for people to not always regard themselves as Catholics even if they are fallen or recovering.

Sadly, if you don't have someone who directs you to another denomination for social reasons, fallen/recovering Catholics are often left alone in the world like orphans who must negotiate the perils of life by their own inward moral compass.

Mudflap has deep faith in the higher powers but he struggles with organized religion.

Just like Mudflap is a conservative in most ways and is even registered as one. But he is struggling more and more everyday with the Republican Party. They are not really true to the conservative ways; they are drifting to a place where the government controls all aspects of everyone's life.

Like Mudflap's mom told him, it's the men running it all, that's the problem. She still had her faith and hung tight to it right to her last moment.

Mudflap is not making judgments just observations.

Mudflap was worried about his character idea being pirated because there are so many Mudflap's with bigger stories, better stories, more righteous, more moral than Little Old Country Boy Mudflap taking on a Pot-Bellied Old Bully of a Captain or an Over-Zealous Bully/Lazy Principal.

Mudflap likes history -- are you guessing where he's going with this?

At the patent office, in the last moments with the adviser, it hit Mudflap like a slap up the side the head. One of the biggest Mudflaps ever was Jesus Christ.

Mudflap says one, only because the story of Jesus is not exactly unique. There are other stories in other cultures of a man who becomes a savior of sorts and follows the same story line of Jesus. Is it reasonable or fair to say the story may have played out before in other times and cultures?

Is it not more unreasonable to think that Jesus only came once, to one people?

Think Universalist! Jesus has been around longer than most people realize.

Politically, Jesus is the biggest common denominator between the extreme rural north, the extreme rural south, the extreme right-wing of the Midwest, the West Coast, and all the inter-connected liberal cities.

Jesus was not a bully and Mudflap highly doubts he would endorse bullies to carry forward his message.

Mudflap thinks liberally but leans conservatively. He likes his Republican-run, conservative small town, but sometimes questions them. He is not thumping the Bible or preaching hell and damnation. He is free spiritually but he's no liberal either.

Nasty, that's the word, just plain "nasty" is what the political climate is like. They are all just as mean as can be. Mr. Coat Hanger frame-of-mind politics. Everyone must bend to the will of whatever party they are in or they will bring chaos to the other side!

You can't preach Jesus and God and then act horribly towards everyone who is of a different race, religion or political affiliation.

How do you all like the hissy fits in politics? Real classy, all drama without a real solid basis. Just theater and bluster to throw attention away from debating the issues. It is a form a bullying.

Mudflap, in his years of doing business with the general public, has seen this kind of behavior before in people who don't want to pay but have a poor or no case for their reason.

Mudflap once worked for a very rich, big hot-shot lawyer named Gutless who thought he was someone very special. This mature, outstanding individual literally clenched his fists and jumped up and down like a spoiled little child would do, crying over $500 dollars.

It was a lot of money (especially at that time) for Mudflap to lose, but he always felt it was well spent as he never had to service the little brat ever again.

Mudflap is no Liberal, they can be nauseating to him. Watching all the spoiled brats who are leading the conservatives makes him want to just plain puke. When they are confronted with facts, they go off on little tirades. Pick a hearing, any hearing; it's always the same tactic, brat-style foot stomping.

"In God we trust" has been ingrained into our political system from the very beginning.

Regardless of whether we say, "You cannot mix Church and State" and the fact that the country was built on the idea that we were escaping the controls of the church, the religious influence on our politics has a solid lock on our country.

One thing I think most of us can agree on is that many of Trump's policies are good, but most people don't like the man himself and, even if they back him, they would not act the same way themselves.

Why do the extreme religious people back an immoral bully? Have they sold their souls to push their agendas?

181

Many of the same people against women's choice are against welfare for struggling mothers. They want to punish women with a fire and brimstone frame of mind.

Mudflap's friends in Maine, true conservatives who are pro-life and stand by their convictions, practice what they preach. They adopt and care for multiple children, extending their family and the values they hold dear. Great people who put their own personal interests and luxuries aside for the good of other people who need help. Mudflaps in their own right.

That's religion in action, not just lip service.

Mudflap, Over and Out !

P.S. Real Time: Can you keep a secret? Do you belong to any Secret Societies? The Catholic Church does do some very good things for the community, and their hospitals are outstanding. With that said, the men running things often spoil the charitable work by bullying the parishioners, and sadly, outright abusing them.

When joining the Knights of Columbus, you are sworn to secrecy and dedication to the organization. Then the men in power bully you and try to run your life. You swear an oath, and they show you "The Box," and you must swear again never to reveal what's inside.

But they abused a friend of Mudflap's who was a "Devout Catholic" and treated him poorly. So, in defiance of the Bullies and disillusioned with the "Church Politics" in general, he slipped into the fallen status and spilled the beans so to speak.

Mudflap swore an oath to no one but his wife, so he is quick to reveal "The Knights' Secret" to his readers. "The Box" has a "little house" inside, described like a little bird house with doors that open, and inside the house is a "Human Skull."

That's the big secret and you're sworn never to tell, but why? Is it because it's illegal to have someone's head in a box? Is there some body parts law? And whose head is it? Maybe it's the last guy who told the secret, or some poor gambler who got in with the wrong bookie.

What's the point of "The Skull?" Why is it in a little house? Is it supposed to represent a "Saint?" I would think they would run out of saints' heads, so it can't be a real saint.

They can't pass it around to all the different groups of Knights, so each one has their own skull? That's a lot of decapitated heads floating around.

Makes you wonder.

MF. Way Over and Under, Out !

P.P.S. Real Time: Mudflap got a letter in the mail, very personalized, from a local Jehovah's Witness in the usual soul-saving format. He replied to the letter and engaged the woman in conversation about trying to focus on pushing out positive messages to our troubled society. She, on the other hand, seemed more happily focused on the turbulence we are experiencing and what she interprets as the End of Days.

Mudflap said to her, "Don't get too happy; the world is not going to end tomorrow. I'm trying to focus on helping people today." She agreed that it wasn't coming tomorrow, but assured him that the time line was clearly in unison with the prophecy.

Jesus is coming, the believers will be saved, and you can't say they didn't try to warn us.

MF.> Out !

HOME POLITICS

Charity Starts at Home.

So does Politics.

You should be politically correct even dealing with your spouse.

If you have problems compromising with your significant other, you have no business trying to push your ideas on your community.

Mudflap, Over and Out !

Mudflap and Wife are in a Yin and Yang-type relationship.

Wife the Liberal, raised as a Quaker (as passive aggressive as they come), will gladly give away the store every chance she gets. She saves spiders while cleaning the house and leaves plenty of places unattended to create habitat for more as she goes.

She is comfortable in clutter and more interested in her book than she is in a sponge. Taking good care of her family, and especially being a good wife, is very important to her. But don't expect her to be too attentive. She is often off in her own little world; her priorities are not necessarily in any efficient-type order. Her decisions are based most often in the moment, and she is easily distracted by flowers, birds, and her appetite. If she's not eating, she's planning the next meal. The upside is she's a great cook and a very thrifty shopper.

In the warm weather she gets lost in her garden; a cluttered country-style so packed with different plants, weeds have to fight to survive. She is not a mulch fan, rather a let-it-all-spread advocate. Flowers follow her around, popping up everywhere. She's a friend of the birds and insects, even going so far as to raise and care for her own group of Monarch Butterfly caterpillars. Spending much of her time checking and fussing over them, elated as they hatch. Then she moves the newly-morphed butterflies to safe spots to dry, protecting them from predatory birds.

Once, a local spiritualist/medium who is renowned in her field said, "Wife is descended from the Fairy World."

I'm not sure one can get more liberal than that.

Mudflap, on the flip side, is an organized clean freak who gets frustrated in clutter and is much more focused in the real world. A concrete sequential with an abstract random point of view, prioritizing everything he can, trying to bring chaos to order.

In the bigger picture they want exactly the same things. The fights they have are only about how to get to the end results.

That's what a good relationship has to have. It doesn't matter which perspective you're coming from, what's more important is that you want the same goals.

When traveling with a partner on the Road of Life, it's ok if you split up and take the scenic routes as long as you meet up at the same destination.

If your partner takes you somewhere off the main road that you weren't expecting to go, quite possibly you may find yourself pleasantly surprised by the experience.

Mudflap, Over and Out

CHAPTER 7

The Moderates

The people in the middle are the ones who get things done.

Like the middle class, the working class, they have to get things done.
That's what they do.

No matter what the color or creed, they combined are the majority.

It's Time to Come Together.

Mudflap, Over and Out !

Mudflap likes his guns and is for background checks. Mudflap loves Jesus, but has big problems with the Catholic Church and any church who put women in second place.

Mudflap thinks women should have equal rights, but he believes in going above and beyond what's necessary, pampering the women in his life, too. That's one reason he is a Mudflap: taking extra good care of the women in his life is his purpose.

We must embrace some contradictions and laugh in the face of others.

Washington, D.C. has been a great experience for Mudflap every time he has ever gone there. Everyone in the country should make a point of going at some time in their lives to see the national treasures that belong to us all.

It's wonderful to see the diversity working together making us a great nation.

Excluding people stifles our growth; exclusion stifles our souls as well.

Mudflap works hard. He likes people who work hard and have standards. He is a tough judge, so his take on effort in the work place is no cheap opinion. As you know, Mudflap can be a real hard-ass when you get him going.

Mudflap's opinion from his experience in Washington is that the black community is doing more for the country then they are getting credit for, at every level. Keeping Washington going and doing a top rate job at it.

Just an observation mind you. They really got it under control and the Jesus is right there with them.

It's something Mudflap has just thrown out there in case any of the Good Old Boys in God's Country had any questions. A big reason you can call yourselves free and play with your tractors out

188

there in the pucker brush is because the Brothers and Sisters got your ass ends covered back in D.C.

The Catholic Church is an easy target these days. Mudflap, ahead of the curve in his usual style, has not liked them since the first quarter he put in their basket.

It seems to Mudflap that all the different factions of the church are more of a problem to the country as a whole, not just the decline in a particular religion's practice.

Any town's social structure is greatly enhanced by healthy, happy, spiritual organizations. On a community level, there is no better source of common pride and decency.

When the churches get so large that their influence is way beyond that of a town, and it becomes as big as an entire state, they create problems. They start working toward their own interests instead of thinking of the country as a whole.

They are all supposed to be working for the same thing. The Muslims, too. Their God is the God of Abraham, the same God as for the Jews and the Christians, the whole pile of them.

That only leaves the peace religions such as Native American, Buddhist, and Hindu. These groups don't seem to be attacking anyone.

Mudflap doesn't like it. They should all be on the same side.

One double standard that Mudflap does not like is: The same conservative right, who do not want back ground checks for gun purchases and less restrictions for all sorts of things, want to police a woman's body. They want to look into our bedrooms and even repress the practice of birth control.

Let me make one thing clear: Mudflap is not pro-abortion, he is pro-choice. There is a big difference.

There are all sorts of situations, and the choice is one that the woman has to live with for the rest of her life.

Mudflap would save every life if he could. He can only say that he was not allowed a choice but has lived with the pain of a choice that was not his to make.

If the church wants to give counsel to women in need, that is their right, and I'm sure they feel it's their duty, but they must draw the line when it comes to forcing anyone to do anything. The church is there to guide not to demand. Free will is the will of God. Only God can judge not the clergymen.

If there are unwanted children born, the extreme conservative right does not want to give any aid to that child who had no choice in any of it. And they are anti-Planned Parenthood, too? Really? Planned Parenthood does a lot more than abortion, they give affordable health care. After Mudflap's children were born, and for many years that followed, his wife got all her feminine heath care done through Planned Parenthood.

Not giving aid to children and mothers in need is outright cruel, isn't that what The Jesus would say? What would The Jesus say about the shooting of people at Planned Parenthood? And the closing of their offices, cutting off the aid to the poor and less fortunate. If you want to force women to have children, then morally, you should help care for that child.

The double standard rules of many extreme religious people lack compassion.

Somewhere the church dogma points a finger, like the Grand Inquisitor, fueling the actions of hate and the extremists.

The finger of hate is not the finger of The Jesus.

Jesus is the hands of love and compassion, Mohammed, too!

The Jews should not be immune: No church is completely without fault, but the Jews are still sore from being the total Mudflaps of the Second World War, the last part of the twentieth century and now into the new millennium.

Mudflap can relate to the Jews like being little brothers; they are seasoned at being beat up. They are scrappy and quick to defend themselves. You have to cut them some slack.

Mel Gibson didn't get that memo. He can scream out his anger down under somewhere in isolation.

He is a perfect example of the extreme and what it does to the minds of the people they support.

Mudflap always thought Gibson could not stop being Mad Max, his original character. In all his movies from the Lethal Weapon series, to *Patriot* and *Braveheart*, he is just Mad Max. And that Passion movie? Mudflap couldn't watch it after seeing some short cuts. He, like many other extremists, wallows in pain and loves to spread it around.

Apocalypto is an interesting movie but it's just Mad Max of the jungle.

Good riddance to Gibson. Forty years of Mad Max and we all have had enough.

Back to the extremists, the Mad Maxes of the country.

Smaller government, only when the conservative right wants it smaller. Bigger and more overshadowing, as bad as the dreaded Nazi's, when they want to push their agendas onto others.

Mudflap's got one for ya: remember the infamous lady with the six kids?

Well, she obviously was no fan of men who leave their families. Once, on a little rant of her own, she went off about the Buddha. He left his wife and child to wander the world and find himself. "Hell," she said, "find himself? He should have thought about finding himself before knocking her up!"

"It's a whole religion based on a guy who left his family." She went on and on.

So there Buddha, under the bus you go!

Now, as long as the Hindus keep their Karma good, the Native Americans stay quiet, and all the children of Abraham don't squabble between each other, you would think we would all be good to go, wouldn't ya.

But we are not, we are not good to go at all. The country is more divided than ever.

Mudflap confesses his wife is a total liberal. She, the Sweet Little Thing, will gladly give away the store. Mudflap is the more Yang side of the Yin. He is not as sweet or as nice as she is, anyone who knows them will testify to that fact.

But actually, Mudflap is nicer because he tells you what he thinks and you know where you stand.

The slow and painful ways of the passive aggressive are not easy to deal with. The anguish, and its long drawn out torture, is not very nice at all. The liberals like to dish out their pain as well, it's just a different cuisine.

So, to all the Liberals too far to the left, we will just get a tow rope and drag you behind the bus.

Each special interest group only seeing their side, it gets old.

Mudflap's statement "you can't separate Church and State" does appear to be true.

But it's not necessarily a bad thing, we should just go with the current and flow to the center.

Our security is diversity and inclusion, bringing more people together.

Just like giving a little slack to children as they mature, letting goodness guide their way.

Let's not be the "No" type parents, like Mr. Coat Hanger, who cultivate pain, fear and hate.

Security is the soft hand of the left (a kinder and gentler machine gun hand), not the hard boot of the right.

We have to embrace that we are liberal and conservative. Let's not forget it was white America that voted in the first black president, twice. That proves that the majority of the country is moderate. Obama did not push the black agenda hard on the country, he tried to be everyone's president. The extreme right abused not only Obama but the country as a whole. Not getting the work done they were being paid to do. Wasting time with the obstruction crap they love so much. Time and again you would hear of them shooting down things that they were for in other bills, just to be confrontational. They acted like spoiled children, foot-stomping babies. And the left in the prior eight years spent their time pounding George W. Bush, in retaliation and anger from the cycle before that as the right had spent eight years pounding Clinton.

Jumping ahead, it's the left's turn again to go after Trump who would not have gotten elected in the first place if the politicians were doing their jobs. And it didn't help that the Democrats pushed Hillary on us. (In a warped DNC conspiracy.)

Ever notice, in most elections you vote against someone instead of for a person and/or you vote for whichever one is the lesser of the two evils?

Three decades of back and forth harassment while the business of moving the country forward for the common good of all the people is not getting done.

Is it ever going to stop?

The climate is an alarm clock trying to wake us up, but too many of us have been on a bender, and the alarm is ringing through a hazy fog like in a drunken fool's head on a Monday morning.

Theodore Roosevelt and the progressive era was a period of social activism and political reform, addressing problems caused by industrialization, urbanization, and immigration. Things we still are dealing with today. Teddy also went after political corruption, not letting the bullies run the system. And he was pro-women, addressing their right to vote through the women's suffrage movement.

Teddy was a true advocate for the environment, doubling the number of sites in the National Park System.

"Speak softly and carry a big stick."

They all should take a hint from that quote. Quiet down and pull that stick out, it's not to sit on!

Mudflap, Over and Out !

P.S. Real Time: Double standards in play again. Demonstrations start against the lock down and sequester of the masses. A religious group congregate on the beach and make a point to show the shaking of hands in defiance of social distancing. (If it's "End of Days," they welcome it.)

More far-right people demonstrate with signage that reads, "My Body My Choice" combined with Trump 2020." They are against sequestering and work place lock-downs.

"My Body My Choice?" Isn't that the women's slogan of the "Pro-Choice?"

You have to give them credit for being consistent, even if it's "consistently selfish and crazy."

MF. Over and Out !

Jay Alden Bailey

DRIVING IN CONNECTICUT

Connecticut gets a bad rap for being cold. Not only weather-wise, but socially, and it's even considered to be a rude environment. I would more accurately describe the state's social demeanor as skeptical and private. I would say you could just call us "Cool." Last I knew, that's a good thing to be.

If you want to criticize the state's people, I would be on board when it comes to the open road and the drivers on it. No question here, Connecticut can be among the worst of the worst.

Be careful driving through the state; you are taking your life in your hands.

Half the drivers are just trying to survive, the other half are split into four factions:

#1 The Complacent: On the phone or otherwise not paying attention.
#2 The Completely Aggressive: On your ass, ready to run you off the road, better get the hell out-of-the-way crowd.
#3 The Combination: Flying along, weaving through traffic, on your ass, ready to wipe you off the road, while on the phone, too.
#4 The Righteous: They don't speed and make a point of getting in the way of everybody they can.

All four groups are capable of road rage if you dare them.

Mudflap's advice is: Keep your hands on 10 and 2, pay close attention, and just go with "The Moderate Flow."
Over and Out !

Connecticut is a very innovative state. At one time, there were more patents coming out of Connecticut than any other state in the country and any other country in the world. Connecticut has been ahead of the curve since the beginning of our great nation.

May 21st. 1901: Connecticut was the first state to pass a driving-law package that included speed limits: 12 miles per hour in the city and 15 miles per hour in the country. The law also included slowing down for intersections and giving right of way to horse-drawn carriages.

CHAPTER 8

Mother Earth

We cannot leave out the Pagans. They were here first.

In New England, it is all about precedence.

The Mayflower crowd had to turn on the Indians, so they could claim to be here first.

That was just plain cheating.

Mudflap, Over and Out !

The Christian faith is full of Pagans, but it's ok, they are saved too. You can believe in both.

Jesus teaches love not exclusion.

Think like a Universalist: In the church's beginning it was the goal to incorporate the Pagan beliefs into the system.

It's not just a coincidence that Sunday is a holiday and Christmas is on the winter festival, as well as Easter on the spring re-birth festival. There are more similarities such as the May Pole Dance and so on. You can be a Child of God and the Earth and love Jesus, too.

The story we know today and celebrate is a customized version to incorporate the Pagans into Christianity. (That's why the Orthodox Christians and Jews consider Saturday the Sabbath.)

When the Roman Catholic Church was building and expanding, they knew enough to include as many people as possible, diversifying their congregation. Strengthening the population with inclusion and love, that is the Jesus message.

Maybe the conservative right wants to ignore Mother Earth but you don't need a prophet to show you what's happening. The Earth refuses to be ignored and is retaliating against us. We must clean up our act and our planet before it's too late.

There are those who wish to rush in the rapture, ruin the planet, and get it over with. Like a drunk who has had too much to drink and finishes the rest of the bottle anyway.

The Native Americans' spiritual culture was close to the earth and they lived in harmony with nature. They lived with the land; we live on it. All we need to do is start taking the tips from the old ways. Supporting green energy, farming local, and urban gardens will help everyone live with nature in some fashion.

Is Christianity clearly one God as they preach? Or are there gods like the Greeks? Was Christ a Demi-God who rose to God status, now making two? And Mother Mary has been elevated also; it's not really any different than the "Gods of old."

199

The Christians stole the holy trinity idea from the Pagans -- the divine feminine, divine masculine, and creation.

Something Mudflap has always wondered about: Who is this "Holy Ghost?" This guy creeping around, what is he really? God's Henchman, the Soul Sheriff looking in your bedroom and in the closet of your mind? Is it a God of sorts, too? Or is he just a spy and a rat. We executed spies. Nobody likes them. Let's not leave women out. Maybe the Holy Ghost is a she. Who, or whatever this thing is, makes you wonder.

If you're a good native, way out in your isolated world away from civilization, and you are good to your people and your family while believing deeply in a great spirit, how could God possibly condemn you when the only thing you have at fault is a different geography and a different culture?

What supreme being would send a pure soul to eternal damnation?

A Bully is what God would have to be to take sides.

In the Church there should not be bullies: the men bullying men, demeaning women, and wanting control and power over all.

The few people that live in jungles, mountains, or isolated islands are more likely truly connected to the greater powers that be. They are immaculate in the eyes of God.

Civilization can't help being corrupt, like absolute power.

Did you know at the end of a good Catholic's life, the priest is more concerned about what the church is going to get out of them financially above their last rites and services? It's a very sad fact, one the church should be just as sorry about as the sexual abuse thing.

I know for a fact multiple circumstances where priests didn't have time for the dying. (Saying how busy they were.) Literally asking for the money to give the last rites and these were regular church supporters who gave throughout their entire lives.

Hey, you're about to drop dead. We need one last payment out of you.

They really have got a big bag of issues.

How about that living in poverty thing: Every church building, rectories and all, that Mudflap has ever seen are full of wealth, comfort, and/or splendor. Mudflap would love to live in that kinda poverty and they don't have to do the maintenance. The priests just walk around smiling and blessing, what a racket.

To throw the Catholics a bone, they do a lot of good work at their hospitals. Any hospital with a St. in front of the name is doing good work in the community. If the poor go there, they don't get chased after for the bill like the industrialized hospitals would do.

There are some good priests and sisters just like there are some good realtors.

They are trying to speak out: In Washington, DC. on a local news channel, Mudflap heard the story of a sister who was speaking against the Church's hypocrisy. I noticed her story got squashed.

God is not in the clouds or in space. God is here in every form of life on the planet.

Remember, it's all about setting precedence. And:
Mother Earth was here first.
Mudflap, Over and Out !

P.S. Real Time: The Coronavirus strikes!
The Earth is speaking loudly. Are people listening now?
MF.> Out !

((((((COINCIDENTALLY, COINCIDENTAL))))))

Mudflap made a point in his first book of addressing "the coincident" as not being properly defined. It is not a random happening. It's the energy in people's minds combined with the greater forces around us connecting.

If you don't ever get a coincidence happening to you once in a while, either you are on the wrong path or just aren't paying attention.

That *deja vu* moment and/or the coincidence is saying that you are in the spot you are supposed to be. It's a good thing, or it could be a warning.

Pay attention and keep connected.

Mudflap, Over and Out !

Connecticut is a Native American word for "long river place". It's core word in English is connect, and rivers are connections. We are all connected.
MF.> Out !

CHAPTER 9

Revolution

"Let he who is without sin cast the first stone."
Jesus, AD. Stopping the mob-killing of a woman.

"Ours is not to reason why. Ours is but to do and die."
The Charge of the Light Brigade. 1854, Alfred Lord Tennyson

"I have not yet begun to fight!"
John Paul Jones, 1779. On the deck of his ship replying to the request that he surrender.

Prophets, Poets, and Heroes Transcend Time

All Revolutionaries.

Mudflap, Over and Out !

Washington, D.C. February 2019: Mudflap woke up slowly in his hotel room on the day he would get to play tourist and have that time he had promised to his Sweet Wife; the copyright and trademark work was behind them.

He sat in the bed drinking a paper cup of coffee from the room's mini coffee maker. The news was on the TV, and he was trying to have a routine morning even though his last month had been anything but routine.

Mudflap's Sweet Wife makes him coffee every morning and brings it to him in bed, spoiling him for that moment. Once he gets up, it is non-stop work.

Watching the news and weather, he sips his coffee and mentally prepares himself for the conditions ahead of him.

Cursing the weathermen for their over-zealous hype, he then gets up and proceeds to prepare for the day's battle ahead. Now it's his turn, his efforts spoil the wife for the rest of her day.

Mudflap was not looking for trouble, he was thinking about a nice day at the Federal Mall. The weather was on their side, and they were slipping in and out of Washington between storms.

Mudflap sat there thinking about his prior day in negotiating the federal offices and how impressed he was with the quality of the people he had found there. What a great country he was thinking to himself.

Then the news played a terrorist voice recording, threatening civil war if anyone dared to confront the president. "Civil war is not civil," he exclaimed, calling to take up arms against the left.

Mudflap was disgusted by the threat.

(Here we go !)

Mudflap didn't go on about politics or religion in the first book because he wanted to be everybody's Mudflap. He did not want to exclude anyone from his vision of Mudflaps all over doing good things in selfless ways.

Mudflap cannot stay quiet when the line is crossed, the switch flips, and he chooses sides. He is a Republican, but a moderate one and wants to be in the middle, including all. But you have to stand up against Bullies and call them out when you know what's right.

Some people must be excluded, like those who threaten violence against peaceful people. These extremists are not patriots; they are hate-mongers and terrorists.

They are weak and afraid. That's why they spread fear, it's what they know. Remember: "Bullies are scared people hiding inside scary people."

This extremist was daring to tear our great country apart because he was afraid of not getting his way.

Poor, little boy brat is going to stomp his foot in anger and bully everyone.

That's just not going to work here in our free society. If Obama had acted in the same way as Trump, the right would have gone crazy.

Our parents fought the Second World War to stop fascism, yet we are such a free society we still allow the Nazi party to exist. We recognize the right to one's opinion even if we do not agree, even if it's an extreme one.

Violence is where we draw the line. Nobody takes the Nazi party seriously they are just weak little white boys playing dress up.

Nobody is going to put up with them or any other violent extremist. (The repeating Nazi dig is not a typo.)

Once the liberals get going, the right will have trouble on their hands. They won't want heads on pikes, they will demand them.

Like the switch that flips, don't put the liberals' backs against the wall. Bullies win battles, not wars. Look at history I say to the extremist, and see that decency will prevail over oppression.

P.S. Real Time: Trump has peaceful protesters gassed so he can walk across the street to wave a Bible. (Church and State?)

Protests turn violent. ("Bad" for the left side's cause.) The right-wing media harps on violent protesters non-stop. See, nobody likes violence, the Right cries foul.

The Yin and Yang represents balance, a good example for democracy.

There would be no right without the left, that simple fact eludes the conservative movement. Like the old Hermann Hess book of *Siddhartha*: The protagonist, after the many different lives he was exposed to, came to the conclusion that all was good and everything had its place.

Everything happening simultaneously across the world is what makes the world. There could not be bad without the good, or the beautiful without the ugly. The sooner you accept that everyone has their place, the sooner you yourself will find inner peace.

Religion is supposed to be about inner peace and love. The extremists seem to have very little love of mankind or any inner peace at all.

Trump and Sanders are two different sides of the same coin. I am saying Bernie has a lot of good ideas, and we should listen to him, not that he is the right one to bring the country together.

THIS IS A THEORY: The Earth is speaking loudly and we have to pay attention to the polar caps melting. Trump is not the answer but he was a necessity, a step that had to be taken. Had Hillary Clinton won, it would have been status quo and we would have gone along for another eight years without change. Then the Republicans would turn over the White House again and do another eight more years of the status quo. Sixteen years is just too long to push the problems off.

Now, after Trump has "broken the ladder" so to speak, and it's time to "throw away that ladder," maybe a liberal Democrat doesn't seem so outrageous as some people once thought. Many of Bernie's ideas are going into effect in states now. The workforce getting a higher wage and more people paying into the system is not a bad idea. Then they are getting more out of the system that they pay into and it's not welfare. That's economic reform.

It's not welfare if people are working and still need assistance. It's bad laws, because the laws let the companies impoverish their workers. It's bad legislation that lets the big companies keep all the profits and send their workers to get government assistance. Talk about chasing your tail in circles. It's so stupid you have to wonder who is on the take for such policies?

Taxing big companies is not socialism; it's a solid economic foundation for an expanding country, a country which should lead the way of economic prosperity globally, as well as lead the industrialized nations to a cleaner planet.

That should be the future of America, a solid foundation for an expanding world.

Mudflap always thought Bernie should never have used the word free, that makes hard- working middle class people think it's another bill for them. Affordable is the right term; nothing should be free. Everybody should chip in something.

No president gets everything they want. If we elected a liberal, the conservatives would never let them go wild. Through the processes our legislators would keep the country balanced. Bernie Sanders wants the greedy bankers and large corporations to give back to the country like any small business would in a home town. That's not unreasonable thinking, that's plain fair play.

The Greedy Bankers were one of Mudflap's first complaints.

The banking system, in a spiral of greed, kept driving down the interest rates lower and lower. First, they made lots of money refinancing everyone, Mudflap included. Then they took away the interest in your savings. Next step, they started charging you to have money in the bank, "fees galore."

The end result is you have to put your money into a volatile stock market to make any good return. Or, tie up your funds in crappy-paying CDs that penalize your principal if you dare draw the money out. Losing the interest should be penalty enough. No, they want to steal some of your savings outright.

Back to a change:

Mudflap says there is time to fix the environment and the economy with a coordinated green energy industry and an infrastructure repair and development program.

How about the "Oil Industry" leading the way, capitalizing on the green energy as we wean down on fossil fuels? Wake up, Big Oil. Take advantage of your billions, and pave the way with your oily tar, making the money as we drive towards the cleaner roads in the future.

Mudflap has a friend who thinks Trump's impact on our foreign affairs may be irreversible. That's another whole topic that could use a chapter. Mudflap is hoping that foreign affairs will smooth themselves out once the Trump cycle is over.

How about more urban agriculture and tax breaks for small local farms? Reduce transport of foods long distances while increasing the quality of the food itself, making more of our areas in the country self-sustainable; and many other, if Mudflap dares to say "socially expanded programs" which will create jobs and support more expanding.

We have a dangerous widow-maker hanging over our heads that Mudflap would like to point out.

Mudflap will keep bringing up self-sustaining regions for a reason. The drastic decline of local farms is a problem. Another one of the government's mistakes is putting our food in the hands of the industrialized farms, giving them incentives, but leaving out the small local farms.

Now follow this idea.

We have become extremely dependent on the Internet to move the country as a whole; nobody can dispute that.

We have very limited access to our food source at a local level.

Are you getting the math?

A crash in the Internet and/or power grid, without a paper back-up or the staff to push the paper, will grind the country to a halt.

It would not take very much time at all for the stores to run out of food. Fuel and all sorts of the necessary commodities would be affected.

Everything is on the digital system; a major power failure would cause havoc.

The old phone system used to work during power failures. No power did not mean no phones. Now that they have gone digital, land lines fail too during outages.

During the big "Halloween Snow Storm" that ravaged the Northeast, Mudflap lost lots of calls on his land and cell phone service. The tree emergency went on longer than any hurricane or ice storm that Mudflap had ever worked though. The smart people kept calling when not receiving replies. Many people were mad at Mudflap, thinking they were ignored when in reality their calls got lost in cyber space.

A major widespread outage could easily cause panic and chaos.

People have become soft and are selfish, they are babies; panic would quickly exacerbate any drastic situation.

Too many eggs in the Internet and power grids baskets, and most of the other eggs are in the industrialized farms' control.

They hold a lot of power over us as everyone clicks the mouse, scrolls their phone, and expects the world to act at their fingertips.

Big business has its place and can be good for the country. We have to get them to take care of the people who are at the bottom, holding the system up, instead of them taking advantage of the population.

We cannot leave out small businesses; they are a huge part of our struggling workforce.

Especially, we must support local farms and make access to local food sources regionalized.

Local is a plus for security, for health, and it's mindful of the pollution associated with transport, pesticides, and preservative issues.

We must stop letting the big companies extort what they want by keeping us in a constant position of neediness and/or fear.

The "revolution is," the "theory is," Trump had to break the system to stop the status quo and reverse our country's direction.

I am not saying that I agree with all that has happened.

I am saying put America on the right path forward.

Mudflap, Over and Out !

P.S. Real Time: Look how quickly people panic. As the Coronavirus struck, the hoarding started instantly. The toilet paper thing proves how insecure and weak people become in a crisis.

There is no lack of household paper products; the problem is the panic and hoarding.

Honestly, if Mudflap really thought there was a commodities shortage and a real end-of-days crisis, toilet paper is not the first thing that comes to mind as a need to have item.

What a bunch of Babies ! ! !
MF. Eyes Rolling and Out !

CHAPTER 10

HIS TRUTH

In God We Trust.

His Truth is Marching on.

God Save the Queen.

It's Ice Water in the Winter for the Rest of You.

Mudflap, Over and Out !

The British have an interesting take on handling the God and Country issue. The Monarch represents the moral consciousness of God, the higher powers that be, and the greater spiritual good of the people. While the Parliament does the work of practical law, where the people have their say as how they are to be governed, taxed, defended, and so on.

That takes a lot of pressure off the Prime Ministers allowing them to spend more time actually governing.

Too bad that the British were so heavy-handed back in the eighteenth century. The Mr. Coat Hanger discipline tactics didn't fare well with the young and independent thinking colonies.

If the colonies had been treated fairly, there would never have been a need for a revolution at all.

The French monarchs might not have lost their heads either. A lot of their economic problems had been caused by financing the colonies' war. The trickle-down politics of change showed little mercy.

The colonies were treated like the young Mudflap on his first jobs where he gave out his all, only to be kicked down.

Young people don't mind starting at the bottom and working up. It's the holding down for greed, status, and personal comforts of their superiors that makes the work experience so unrewarding.

When Mudflap hosted parties for his son and his friends at Pine Island, there was a particular young man who comes to mind. He worked at a bank for minimum wage and was putting a lot of hours in every week. He had been employed there a long while as part-time help during his school years. He asked for time off for the Fourth of July. He had never asked for time off before at all. This was a one-shot time to be with his friends as their senior year wrapped up and everyone was moving forward with their lives.

The supervisor at the bank would not let the poor kid have his moment. It did not matter how many afternoons the boy gave up; the banker was more concerned with the other older employees having time off.

The boy was at the bottom of the ladder and was being kicked down into the mud.

Mudflap The Gloves Come Off

Then later, Mudflap's daughter was doing a yoga retreat: a whole group of young people sharing a house on a vacation. Everyone planned for months in advance. A very close friend of hers and group member from back in her high school days had trouble with his work.

This young man had been on the job for a year and a half, taking up the slack, doing shifts for the older employees so they could do more with their families. He asked for the time off months in advance, time off he deserved. As the trip came closer, the employer decided not to let the guy have his moment. His youth was their ticket to abuse him, muscle him, bully him into cancelling. They were messing with all his friends, his girl, everyone. Each young person could not afford to do the trip alone; it was a group venture. And it was also a special time that was not going to ever repeat.

He was given half the time he asked for only after much fuss and stress. They forgot quickly who covered the shifts and who hadn't had time off in a year and a half. The total greed and abuse of power, treatment that they would not have done to an older employee, is typical of how the young are treated in the work place. Cutting short the trip not only hurt the young man in question, it put a damper on all involved. Mudflap says Karma will strike the abusers hard.

P.S. Real Time: The greedy restaurant owner is now closed down as the Coronavirus rages on. I wonder if he is counting the hours he is forced to take off?

The colonies are a metaphor for the kids and our young work force today. If we don't pay the young a living wage, how can they ever expect to have families? That doesn't sound like a good future to work for. It sounds like a really bad deal to Mudflap.

215

The whole reason Mudflap quit any of his jobs was because the employers refused pay what he was worth. We all talk about having so little back in the 1970s, but the reality is, dollar for dollar we were doing better back then. What kids today have to face are much higher expenses and not much different wages, percentage-wise. It is very difficult for them to even think of getting ahead when they live paycheck to paycheck.

P.P.S. Real Time: How can they stock up on food and supplies to sequester during the Coronavirus lock down when they live hand to mouth?

Big business has boomed in the last 40 years and our economy is doing great, but for us as individuals the math is very different.

Point Being: In a personal economy sense, the common person is no better off, and many are worse off than he/she was 40 years ago. That doesn't sound like progress to Mudflap; that doesn't sound like the American dream at all.

Combined with the burden placed back on the parents having to help the next generation, it's a really dumb, unsustainable economic situation.

How can the big companies get tax breaks and show huge earnings and have a workforce that's operating close or below the poverty line? How is it allowed that the big companies get to keep the money in their pockets and pass the heath care and other social burdens back on the states and federal government? Really?

Mudflap did like it when Trump called out General Motors for trying to ship jobs overseas after receiving the big bailout Obama supported. I guess they changed their minds. You

really have to pay attention all the time, they are all so slippery.

Small businesses have to take good care of the people and other businesses around them. They all interact providing each other goods and services. Big business comes into a town and cares nothing for the community they are buying into, only the bottom line of what they can get from that community.

Like Liberals on a "Merry go Round," here we are back to begging for a "decent wage" or at least a "living wage."

On the subject of the Queen, here is a lady who knows her politics. The Queen has been around for a long while and has seen a lot of change. She knows what it's like to be a Mudflap. She has shouldered a lot in her lifetime. Through social change and chaos, through scandal and intrigue, she knows how to handle herself and the media frenzy around her. You can't pick out one bad quote from that lady.

As a matter of fact, Mudflap dares you to try!

Stiff upper lip, on we go!

Trump should take a few tips form Teddy Roosevelt and the Queen of England.

He's doing an on-the-job training situation. Which is ok for a seasoned businessman who knows how to delegate.

That's where he had me at first. He said, "I will pick the best people to advise me." Sounded good to Mudflap!

His administration turned into another season of The Apprentice. Can anyone deny that fact? Please feel free to let me know you disagree and I will post it on my site.

Trump should have taken more notes from Obama, George W. and Big George, too!

They don't shoot their mouths off. Like the Queen, they stay quiet and say only what's necessary.

Mudflap did hear something that George W. said about Trump, then silence.

Silence is golden: The gold plate of Trump's facade is wearing thin and peeling off.

When we lost Big George, we lost the last president who served from the ground up. He was a war hero and head of the CIA. Would Big George believe Putin over his own intelligence agency? He may have talked to Kim Jong Un. Negotiation was not beneath him. But being cozy? I'm not so sure.

Why don't the people of power look to history?

Hitler was not thinking of Napoleon when he went into Russia. Big mistake! You already got the lesson on bigger bullies in the first book.

Trump does not know how to delegate or lead, he just knows how to be a bully.

His Truth is Marching on!

Truth?

Mudflap, Over and Out !

Little Words have Big Impact

In a free society everyone should be able to speak their minds without fear. This statement seems obvious, but yet, we must think before we speak for a number of reasons.

Embarrassment and ridicule in social situations should be enough to censure oneself. In business, your word should be golden: a bond between each party, once made, unbreakable.

With a lack of common courtesy, our words can devastate others as well as ourselves. If these statements are so self-evident, then why do we have so much tension in society today?

The most destructive of all words is not a particular word itself, it's a use, like a patent of sorts.

The Patents Category is quite broad, consuming and eroding the liberties our forefathers fought for. It's called "The Lie."

The Lie can start small and like a seed can grow into a giant tree.
It can also be already large and transplanted purposely to obtain faster growth.

All our Superheroes stand for the same things and these things are in the same order.

Truth, Justice, and The American Way !

Positive words of truth, reinforced by positive actions, is a simple solution to our problems across the boards in every venue.

Mudflap, Over and Out !

CHAPTER 11

Puppy Power

How can somebody beat up a puppy?

It's all about love.

Mudflap, Over and Out !

There once was a young man to whom Mudflap was very generous. He took him under his wing, giving the young man a better work situation than he had ever experienced. Mudflap was generally very good to him, but alas, he was too young to really appreciate the effort. He was another spoiled millennial who did not know yet the true nature of the evils the young have to face in the work place.

It's always a double-edged sword. Mudflap has learned the hard way. Even though he may care for the young workers, they don't feel the same way in return.

This gets back to an original complaint Mudflap has about the guidance departments in the high schools: they do not give proper recognition to the trades. They put the non-college required industries into such a low worthless category that the young have no respect for the jobs. And worse, there is no respect for an apprenticeship or the time it takes to become a master tradesman.

Even though Mudflap paid the young man well and treated him with respect, the young one thought it was funny to ruin the job and relationship with purposeful inconsideration. His biggest gripe was that Mudflap went to Maine and left him working back in Connecticut, not holding his hand on the job.

So, he made problems for Mudflap, and as a joke, hid away and would not answer his phone, bringing himself down from young man to boy status.

Mudflap went to have a word with the boy who lived at home with his parents. The boy had told many stories about his father and his aggressive behavior. The Boy's father was, Mr. Break-You-in-Half: all shoulders and no neck, never went anywhere without a pistol in his pocket. He considered himself a professional security man.

Knowing the reputation of the family he was going to call on, Mudflap took with him his brand new, tiny puppy Lulu as a puppy-shield of sorts.

With the puppy in his arms, Mudflap knocked on the door.

The Boy was not home but his scary farther was. Mudflap got to vent and tell the father about the boy's inconsiderate behavior.

Mudflap kept noticing the man looking at Lulu and back at Mudflap. There is no question that the puppy, who was so tiny and scruffy, and just as adorable as could be, was holding off any anger this man could possibly produce. His no-neck posture and pistol were no match for Lulu's cuteness. Mudflap left with the air clear never to return.

But he did hear later the father had a lot to say to the boy.

221

Lulu melted the beast, his anger dissolved, he was helpless in the presence of "Pure Puppy Power."

When Mudflap heard Bernie Sanders was running for president again, he cringed and said to his daughter, "Are you kidding? Only the millennials want to hear his free-for-everyone speech again."

Bernie has some very valid points and solutions, not just circle talk, but free college and free health care just sounds like a bill to the older, more experienced middle class. He should have used the word affordable, all good hard-working people respect affordable, that makes sense. Free for all sounds like socialism to the mainstream.

A good idea, too, is rein in Wall Street and Big Banking. They have always hurt everybody they can.

Did you ever hear the old anecdote that when the sun is shining, the bank hands you an umbrella, and as soon as it starts raining, they grab it away from you?

We need to make the banking system do better for small businesses and individuals.

They have to stop penalizing small accounts just for being small.

Having some socialized colleges is not going to put the big schools out of business, but it will make them think about being more competitive when seeking tuitions.

We need more good ideas.

We need more Puppy Power.

**It's all about love.
Mudflap, Over and Out !**

CHAPTER 12

Peace

A state of calm and quiet. Public security under law.

Freedom from disturbing thoughts or emotions.

A state of concord as between persons or governments.

An agreement to end hostilities.

Or Piece

A Part of a Whole, a Fragment. One of a Group, Set, or Mass.

A Single Item.

Jay Alden Bailey

Something made or sold, a Product, a Creative Work.

A Coin or a Firearm.

Peace and Piece are things we all want to have and is something we should all be proud to be.
Mudflap, Over and Out !

There are events in time that you cannot forget if you lived through them. Like John Lennon being gunned down in the street. Mr. Peace himself with his chest full of holes. He was taken away from us by a completely selfish individual who's lack of empathy for the world will forever be a stain on our humanity.

When you put good things forward, the karma and peace people believe that good things keep growing.

Acts of violence against good peaceful people stifle the goodness growing in the world. Simple math. The sooner we focus on the better things we can do as a country, the sooner everybody will be happier, even those who disagree. Peace will bring prosperity and violence will only set us back.

Leaders are fair game, they signed up for criticism when they took the jobs.

Mitch McConnell is an obstructionist.

An Example: He cheated the Democratic party out of the Supreme Court appointment. A reasonable choice made by Obama that partisan politics shot down for no good reason. Merrick Garland was a fair choice. So reasonable in fact, the Republicans wanted him ready to be appointed if Hillary Clinton won, worrying she would appoint someone more liberal.

224

McConnell has even cheated his own party, proud of himself as the "Grim Reaper of Bills," letting legislation die on his desk as he just ignores the work done by the House and Senate.

They keep playing it both ways, and that's where they lose Mudflap. He's not as proud as he used to be of the Republican party; he wants to see change. They must get back to their roots of true conservatism.

Just like Mudflap is not as proud to be a descendant from the Mayflower anymore after finding out just how quickly they turned on the natives who helped them survive in the beginning. But he is still pro New England.

We can start by holding our leaders accountable for their sins against the state and demand retribution. Mitch McConnell is a slug, feeding off the negative side of the country's energy. He had the nerve to brag that obstructing our government from working properly was his proudest moment. Did he ever once consider paying more time and attention to passing some laws that would move the country forward?

How did a person of such poor moral quality ever get to such a high position of power that allows him to hurt the country so much?

Mudflap is no fan of Nancy Pelosi but she has to be admired for standing up to such a large over-whelming force and fighting for what she believes is right.

There is talk of peace behind closed doors. Bits of information are sneaking out, but they all look over their shoulders, afraid. But of who? Maybe they should take a chance and stand up and say what's really on their minds.

Jay Alden Bailey

Of course, they are worried about getting re-elected, pandering to special interests and big money.

It takes brave people to be for peace. We need brave people to stand up to Bullies.

You don't have to like Nancy Pelosi to admire her, she is a fighter, a warrior, and a person for peace.

History will tell who had good positive impact on our society and who was the negative. You will feel better if you choose the right side of history.

Will you choose the people who represent peace? Or will you choose the Grand Inquisitor?

In the 1970s, Frank Zappa's "Slime from the Video" is a funny song that hits the mark on the influence television has on our society.

The song goes like this:
I am gross and perverted
I'm obsessed 'n deranged
I have existed for years
But very little has changed.

I am the tool of the Government
And industry too
For I am destined to rule
And regulate you

I am the best you can get
Have you guessed me yet?
I'm the slime oozin' out
From your TV set.

MSNBC and FOX play the same song on different instruments. They exclude information and put out only what they want you to hear. If you listen to FOX you become pro conservative, and if you listen to MSNBC you become pro liberal.

Inclusion against exclusion.

Peace in the world is our obligation to nurture, not our obligation to police, but we should not turn our backs on allies either.

The president can use emergency or war to side-step congress and make decisions not voted on.

By crying wolf when there is no real emergency is treason. We can't have any one person making decisions alone that affect the whole country. That's the Hitler-style of governing.

Mudflap does like talks with North Korea, talks are better than bombs. But then the talks stopped. Kim Jong Un wants attention, gets antsy, ramps up his threat level and around and around we go in a never-ending circle.

We should stay on Russia's good side as well as China's. We should have teams of diplomats and economists working on common ground ideas, pushing forward fair trade and global environmental solutions for our stressed-out planet.

Hitler did not see the bigger bully in Stalin. Trump's bully tactics may backfire dealing with the likes of Putin and Xi Jinping, China's president for life. Xi has way more time on his side than the rest. China is scary because they are more patient and are playing a long game.

What about Brazil's bully leader Jair Bolsonaro? Wiping out the Amazon Rain Forest? Madness! Only thinking of the short-term buck.

We need all the big shots at the same table, all going away with something to bring back to their people.

Then and only then do we have hope for peace and be able to enjoy our piece of the world.

Mudflap, Over and Out !

P.S. Real Time: Russia passes new law making it possible for Putin to remain in power into the 2030s. They are keeping pace with China, making room for their strongman to stay in power.

CHAPTER 13

The Earth is Crying

Round them up, Cowboys

Teddy Roosevelt is turning in his grave as the conservatives drop restrictions.

"Ya-Hoo!" It's a free for all !

Or is it ?

Mudflap, Over and Out !

Isn't it great that you can just jump in a plane and zoom all over the planet and at an affordable price for the masses? But what about the hidden costs associated with the frivolity of spending the planet's resources in such a way.

People should be thinking more greenly for vacations as well as for their necessity-related energy costs.

Here is where Mudflap is not going to make friends, even with the planet's activists. So many people love their fly-away escapes. Like Mudflap's daughter, she is the little "Flower Child." She loves the planet, hates Monsanto, loves Bernie and loves to fly away to tropical places, too. She can't really afford it but manages to figure out ways she can get there.

Even the biggest planet-lover Mudflap knows defends jumping on planes for what Mudflap calls a "Ha-Ha."

Mudflap feels really lonely out there in the Anti-Aircraft Save The Energy Club. He is President, Founder and Sole Member accepting membership applications upon request.

P.S. Real Time: "The Coronavirus Strikes America." Mudflap wrote this chapter way back in March 2019 while his wife and daughter both flew away to exotic places. He had already finished his first book and, while still in the middle of recovery from surgery, he started Mudflap II.

Mudflap at first was not going to go on and on about all the other issues he has with world travel.

But "loose commerce behavior" causes negative effects on the environment. Like the Ash trees being attacked by the Asian Long-Horned Beetle. The bug was brought in on shipping pallets. Without natural predators in the area, the trees are defenseless and are being wiped out. But in the world today, companies care only about fast profits. Just like the Mouse-Clicking Realtors, who disregard the negative effects of driving down the long-term market for the quick buck today.

Well, it's not just a bunch of trees who will die now! Everybody happy? Satisfied? Still think it's good traveling around the planet? Everybody loosely regarding the environment and the negative effects of moving around diseases?

There was a party in Westport Connecticut, the Coronavirus was there, too, with the other party guests. The group dispersed and some flew away to other party venues. They brought the virus many places, even as far as South Africa. Good job, party goers! Bring your fun around the world, fast!

Now who wants to join the Anti-Aircraft Save Energy and the World Club?

Now that I have you in the right frame of mind, maybe you will accept some of my ideas and try to give in somewhere. Stay closer to home on your vacations and start caring more about the world as a whole.

Let's try Monsanto and RoundUp for starters, poison on the plants we eat. You can read about it for hours on the Internet. One thing that jumped out at me when I did a little research was a "Bully article." Where Monsanto sent a guy into an old-time country store in of all places Eagleville, Missouri, to harass and threaten the long-time owner. Eagleville is an out-of-the-way outpost of true American freedom, as tiny a place they could possibly pick on.

"Who's Next?"

There's that "Bullying Thing" again, so popular with the mainstream big business and the far right.

Mudflap can't help but see the bullies everywhere. The dropping of regulations is an assault on the earth.

231

Jay Alden Bailey

P.S. Real Time: Mudflap heard Monsanto sold out the RoundUp business, and chemicals. They sold the liabilities, too. Boy, are they crafty or what?

Mudflap's not a geologist, but he has issues with stuff like drilling and fracking in all sorts of places.

One is, what's it doing to ground water aquifers?

Another is, how it is affecting faults?

Is it going to wake up "Yellow Stone?"

There's a good one! Wake up that "Super Volcano"!

That's something that sure would take the suspense out of things.

Now we know the ocean is dying in sections; Jacques Cousteau tried to warn us long ago as he saw the signs.

Industry is hurting the oceans and we have to be on it.

What industrialized farming and oil drilling are doing to the land, combined with the ocean pollution issues can fill volumes of text.

Then you add dropping regulations on top of it all and we are shooting ourselves in the foot with a shot gun. Our actions are becoming a permanent injury. Sadly, that's too optimistic, it's more like suicide!

Mudflap's daughter wants him to mention factory meat farms and the pollution they cause to water and the methane/carbon dioxide

232

that's put into the air. The industry is compounding the problem by exporting the practice to other countries around the world.

Mudflap gets it, got to feed the people and it is big money fast. Doesn't matter how good it is long term.

Like the bad realtors, it's all about the "fast buck now!" Worry about it later, later.

It's a job for a new Super Hero. Mudflap calls him "Captain Tomorrow."

Actually, Captain Tomorrow is a real person Mudflap knows. He has been dubbed "Captain Tomorrow" because, when overwhelmed, he just throws up his hands and says tomorrow and the problem is solved. It really works quite well if you don't care about where that leaves you in the future because there is always another tomorrow! It's brilliant and stupid all at once.

It would be really funny except the conservative Right's Navy is being led into battle by Captain Tomorrow, and he's not even an Admiral. Kinda like we are being led by a president who is not presidential and didn't really expect to win. He was just having fun shaking up the Republicans.

"Hello." We got in a lot deeper than a lot of us want to admit.

The effects of all the bad climate/pollution decisions compiled up on the planet over the short time since the start of industrial revolution will take a millennium to correct if we start paying attention now.

The compounding effect of non-action will add thousands of years more to the recovery.

The sad reality is we have lost too much time already and have lost too many species of plants and animals.

The damage is already irreversible.

We are not only working with a breakdown maintenance-mentality, it's turning more into a salvage operation.

Yes, my friends, the Earth is crying.

And be aware! She is fighting back, too!
Mudflap, Over and Out !

A Native American Proverb:

We do not inherit the Earth from our ancestors, we borrow it from our children.

CHAPTER 14

The Bigger Church of the World

The Universalist

History should teach us:

The Visigoths Loved Rome and Wanted to be Part of Rome.

The Promise of Inclusion without Resolve, created Despair.

Then they sacked the place !

Let history be our guide. Do we really have to keep learning the hard way?

Mudflap, Over and Out !

Nobody likes to compromise, but the reality is we have to and do most of the time anyway. Only the very few get everything they want. Mudflap has seen spoiled people that do get everything and still aren't happy.

Big church and big government have a lot in common. They both promise a lot and then give as little as possible.

Mudflap was a fan of George H. Bush and believed in the trickle-down Republican "Voodoo Economics." He worked hard, invested in real estate, and believed that the hills and valleys of recession was just a common correction in the ever-rising costs of everything.

Almost 40 years later it is disappointing to see the stagnation of property values in the Northeast. Here's where Mudflap observes little positive growth after a lifetime of work. Backing big business did not create the trickle-down wealth promised. The idea was good, but the greedy, after capitalizing on the system, balked at paying out the wages earned by the masses. They kept finding ways to stall and not pay out for years and into decades.

Mudflap grew up believing the way to wealth was property. Every wealthy person he knew had real estate. He believed in the Republican way. But now he only holds property that costs him to carry with little rise in value.

Mudflap spent what little savings he had on education for his children. His son could not get a scholarship based on need because Mudflap had property. It did not matter to the colleges if Mudflap had to sell at a loss, they wanted to be paid regardless of Mudflap's ability to sustain his future. And now, time is running out to see any benefits the trickle-down effect policy would ever grant.

He sees now, because the top is stingy with watering the plants, that the trickle dries up before anything can grow. We must treat the economy by watering the ground and letting it grow up. Then we will have a self-sustaining system that will keep growing and feed itself.

Big churches act in the same way as big business. They dish out big promises and talk of inclusion and are the most intolerant of all institutions. Where they are supposed to be leaders, loving the masses, they are separatists and create bigger problems.

If you don't believe in the God they believe in, you are evil. Every faction thinks their view of God is the right one.

That's just plain crazy, like the isolated tribesmen, we are talking geography, culture, and language. The verbal word is a huge instant barrier when mixing the masses. Even our own languages have dialects for regions, creating barriers even within cultures. Flatlanders and Yankee Boys within the same race. Diversity is simply not tolerated by some at all.

We will never live in John Lennon's "Imagine" where there is no church or state, no greed or hunger, that's fantasy. But we can be all inclusive and compassionate towards people outside of our accepted social circles.

That's what a bigger world-view of the church should be. Your way is good for the people in your circles and the others are good, too. Nobody is wrong, they just speak a different language, even within the same language and within individual minds.

The Right Wing is afraid of communism, afraid of Bernie, but insist you do it their way, their own form of a communist attitude. We all must conform to their view of God and Country and their view of who is right and wrong.

They want independence and small government only until it does not suit them. Then they turn Commie on us, and then extremists threaten civil war. Obviously, a young soul. This civil war advocate who does not know the real cost of his rhetoric, the boy needs a lesson.

237

The Unitarian Universalist is not at all a new idea. Advocates fought in the revolution and were at the signing of the Declaration of Independence. One of the first Unitarian churches was in South Carolina and its origins can be traced back to the 4th and 5th centuries.

Are we in modern times or a dark age?

Like Liberals on a Merry-go-Round, the conservatives have a favorite horse to ride, too.

It's all about greed, selfishness, intolerance, and power.

The extremists have to let it go and give the country a break, a break it needs and deserves.

Doesn't that sound familiar? Like those employers who wouldn't give the loyal young workers a simple break. And a raise was not even the issue. Bad enough they have the young working for cheap, they don't want to even let them have a life at all. Sounds like a form of slavery. Isn't that what they really want, to own the help and tell them when to breathe.

It's time to realize through our young, God speaks. We must take care of our young and make them strong, not beat them into submission. There are a few powerful people who want to make the masses patsies. We are here to serve the few and the mighty. That's the kind of thinking that will destroy everything that we have worked for in the last 250 years of America.

Watch, you will see the true patriots come to the plate, coming up to try and fix the mess we are in.

We must pay attention closely to the choices.

Will you be a Universalist? Or on the side of the Grand Inquisitor?
Mudflap, Over and Out

CHAPTER 15

Solutions

It's easy to criticize.
It takes more to come up with something positive.

A famous quote:
"You miss 100% of the shots you don't take."
Gretzky

We need more than a couple of shots; we need a lot of rapid-fire!

Mudflap, Over and Out !

Mudflap has a few ideas, not just critical slander, that's easy. Solutions take more thought.

It would be good to have a liberal-thinking president backed up by a conservative, practical, economic-wise group of statesmen who will implement the liberal polices with a conservative approach. But not obstruct the liberal vision, just rein in any overzealous ideas and keep them practical. That way of thinking might actually work for America.

We as Americans are conservative and liberal, that's what makes us great, that's what makes us the true America our forefathers fought for. We are and always will be a great nation, we just have to stop cheating our work force out of the simple securities they spend their lives to obtain.

The meat industries are big polluters and over-doing meat in the diet is not really that healthy. Supporting local farms would decrease pollution and increase the quality of the meat. So simple. We reduce the amount of meat we eat, and what we do eat is better for us, and we become more regionally self-sufficient.

More local farms everywhere with tax incentives, increasing quality, and again, each region is self-sustaining. Agriculture in urban areas, rooftop farms, vacant lots, and even inside growing environments, all to make self-sustaining regions and simultaneously producing higher quality foods. Urban agriculture could also create jobs in cities where jobless rates are higher than the national average, not only lowering the jobless rate, but creating agricultural skills that can become like trades and can be enhanced in many ways.

Each region becoming more self-sufficient and reducing transportation costs. Stop the shipping of under-developed fruits and vegetables, with pesticides and preservatives, and reduce pollution in the process.

America should be in the lead switching over to green energy instead of being behind where we seem to be now. There are other countries ahead of us. We let the big businesses tell us what to do instead of the reverse.

The big petroleum companies should see the writing on the wall and use their resources to lead the switchover. Rather than be threatened by the competition, they should embrace the new technology and be the ones to profit from it.

All business, big and small, should get tax breaks to better care for their employees. The employees should be treated like dependents, not under paid and thrown back at the government for economic relief.

A good place big companies can help society as a whole is to use the vast extra money they hold back and spend it helping with family issues. They can really make a difference and have a positive effect on their workforce.

First pay them enough to be able to have a family. Then:

Increase the quality of the family life with pregnancy leaves. Children from birth to age four are in the most critical years for mental development. Mothers or fathers at home during this critical stage will produce better citizens with proper social development leading to less behavior problems across the boards.

Just like the farms, we should go back to the land with parenting, not industrialized child care, warping our next generation's concept of the world around them. Daycare has become a big industry and has many heartless aspects. The poor amount of attention paid to children is one thing. The parents are under stress to pay and be on a vigorous time schedule. School days off and weather issues don't matter to the industrialized day care. Parents pay dearly, have to snap to it, and have to keep up with the demands of the daycare institutions. You are lucky if you get a good daycare place to do business with.

When addressing big companies, their work force is huge and has a severe impact on our economy. Again, treat the workers like dependents. Give the big companies tax breaks but then force them to pay out wages that sustain their people. They can't leave everyone broke, run with the money, and have the government pick up the slack. That's plain insane!

Mudflap is pro-fossil fuel. It's a necessity. But we need to morph from fossil fuel to green energy at a rate that sustains us as it goes. Exit plan fossil, enter green energy, sensibly.

Reduce government subsidies on the corn industry's junk food that causes health issues and drives up healthcare costs.

If they want to make fuel from corn that may be part of the switchover plan as we exit the fossil fuel dependence.

Fun Facts:
1) The same money value is paid out at minimum wage as the1970s but the top percents' income has exploded.
2) Junk foods cause dire health issues. Hospitals feed the dying, sick and recovering people junk foods.
3) We as a nation are just as poor as we were in the 1970s.
4) Wealth is an illusion for most of the working population. All they have are their comforts and the ease of a high-tech lifestyle with very little long-term security.

The Internet and power grid are the perfect storm, poised to pound us back into the stone age. Make back-up systems with green energy, localized, the same way as the food sources should be.

Every state should be able to sustain itself through any long-term emergency.

The extra food we produce in our industrialized farms could be exported to strengthen our economy and boost our trade deficits around the world. We could help the world by being stronger ourselves.

Build and repair our infrastructure as we strengthen our country. It will be easier to help our neighboring countries and our allies if we are not putting our citizens behind in the process.

As we become stronger and more independent in all these areas, the less risks we will have coping with natural disasters which we know are going to continue and being ready is important.

Just like America helping other countries, if each state is self-sufficient, they can aid each other in crisis.

That kinda thinking is leadership that starts in the community, then it rises to the state, to the nation, and ultimately to the world.

We always want to help everyone around the world and many turn to America in times of crisis. The stronger we are taking care of ourselves, the better we can do for the planet as a whole.

Mudflap, Over and Out !

P.S. Real Time: Mudflap wrote this chapter more than a year before the Coronavirus locked down America.

"Just sayin."

MF. Over and Out !

Jay Alden Bailey

WRAP UP

WHERE ARE WE GOING ?

WHO WILL LEAD US ?

WHO WILL OBSTRUCT US ?

WHO WILL BE HEROES ?

WHO WILL BE VILLAINS ?

AMERICA BE AWARE.

DON'T LET FEAR STOP PROGRESS.

GET INVOLVED.

DO SOMETHING POSITIVE, EVEN IF IT'S SMALL.

When it comes to reforming social and economic issues politically, the first laws passed are not always perfect. Legislation works by agreeing on common-ground topics and making solid footing for the next step. De-regulation, for example, in the wrong areas is a step backward in the care and preservation of our environment.

Change the World and help keep us moving in the right direction.

"ALWAYS FORWARD"

Mudflap, Over and Out !

Epilogue

The old saying: "Do a good deed every day." You can also: "Do a chore every day, too."

How about a combination of both:
"Look through someone else's perspective every day."

You might find it surprisingly enlightening.

MF.

The Alternative Prologue

Mudflap and Sweet Wife were standing by the door exiting the Patent and Trademark Office. They spent a last moment in conversation with the office advisor handling their file. This woman was a clear and steadfast representative of our government, professional in every way. Her reflection and understanding of what Mudflap stands for, combined with her empathy and compassion, obviously deep-rooted in faith, truly humbled and inspired Mudflap.

The Alternative Prologue Story

The point of the original book is that Mudflap is one of many, many Mudflaps everywhere. It's way bigger than this little old, country boy Mudflap.

He looked up mudflap on the Internet. Almost nothing came up at all except, of course, mudflaps. He researched copyrighting the idea and found out you can't just grab up a name and copyright it. You have to develop the idea or character first.

That part was easy because Mudflap is a Mudflap.

But the energy and the connecting circles of the coincidence were about to take hold of him and take him to another place.

Mudflap had recent experiences that were altering his thoughts.

Mudflap had developed a mission since his visit to Washington, D.C.

The copyright and trademark process was enlightening at many different levels. From the virtual world of the Internet to the tangible trip itself, right through the whole experience.

In D.C., Mudflap's wife was on her smartphone navigating the trip. Mudflap is a flip phone guy. She was getting frustrated with her phone. So, Mudflap started asking people in the street for directions and got quicker responses from pedestrians than wife could get playing with her phone.

Mudflap found the people very friendly and generally glad to be of help.

The office they needed to see was on a lower level with an elevator that had only one stop. Most sections were highly secured with desks and security guards everywhere. You could feel the importance of the place in the air.

The Patent and Trademark Office had a small receiving area. Two women receptionists sat behind glass and the room had a modest seating area, obviously not a lot of walk-in traffic.

It didn't take long until another woman came out to help. She listened to Mudflap and his explanation of his intent to market Mudflap as a character. Everything was going well until the paperwork turned electronic.

At the Library of Congress there was a computer for the general public to login with and Mudflap had his manuscript. They didn't need his electronic files. When Mudflap offered his flash drive to the lady there she said simply, "It's not necessary."

At the Patent and Trademark Office there was no computer for the general public. They were not used to walk-in traffic in any great volume. All of a sudden, the reality of the flash drive came sharply into focus. There was no way anyone was going to plug any flash drive into any government computer, period. The headlights were on now, Mudflap had to get paper files. The only paper work he had was left in the truck all the way back at the hotel.

Now it was getting past lunch time on Friday, the hustle was on.

As he sat in the first train, his mind raced through the details; the math was bad, he didn't need algebra to figure out the hotel was just too far.

Mudflap started looking around the train and spotted an interesting looking lady. He approached her and asked her if she

251

knew a place where he could get paper copies of files off his flash drive.

Like a Guardian Angel she rose up to the occasion. She was very outgoing and, with a heavy accent, said she knew just the place and would take Mudflap and wife there personally. She told the Mudflaps stories of her many years of experiences living in Washington and originally being from Barcelona.

She acted as a personal guide and was so lovely to converse with. She brought the couple right into the store and, like an old friend, she left them both with a hug and kiss on the cheek.

She truly saved the day.

As the Mudflaps fumbled around the self-help printer, a store technician came to their aid and was of great help, too.

Along the way, everyone they met was doing a great job and was as pleasant as could be. They were back at the trade office again ahead of the day once more. The lady taking care of their file came back out and spent the rest of the afternoon with them. She gave them a quality experience and advice that turned out to be worth all the troubles.

As Mudflap, wife, and the advisor lady stood at the door in the last moments of their experience, the conversation turned a bit more philosophical. Mudflap began to realize that this woman who was helping them was connected deeply to the powers that be and to our country, everybody in it, her family and to God. She knew what it was to be a Mudflap. She not only created respect for her office and position but restored a faith in Mudflap he had lost long ago.

Those last moments with her were truly inspiring.

She never said a word about religion and did not attempt to preach at all. But God spoke loudly through her, along with her expressions and the content of her conversation. This Lady is an extremely high-quality individual and it was making Mudflap connect the dots.

On the way back, at the train station, the Mudflaps met another interesting young lady. They struck up a conversation while waiting and the couple spent part of the train ride with her. She was a Navy engineer working on jets. When the subject of flash drives came up, she told them how someone would be fired if caught with one. Flash drives are a huge government no-no. And, coincidently, the Young Lady knew a fellow who liked to call himself Mudflap but did not really know why; it just stuck in his head and he thought it was cool nickname.

What a day! They were glad to get back to the hotel for dinner/snacks in the room and an early bedtime.

With business under their belts, Saturday it was back to the National Mall as tourists.

Mudflap was seasoned at the train thing now and he was starting to pay attention more to the people around him. He noticed that everyone was alert and doing their jobs with a true sense of purpose. From the stations, through the streets, security in and around all the buildings, as well as the staff members in the buildings themselves, the city ran like a finely-tuned machine.

Being a country boy, isolated in many ways, Mudflap couldn't help but notice the diversity of the people. It started to make him think about how all sorts of different areas everywhere in the country were all just as isolated. All different ecosystems working together as one big organism.

In the morning of his departure, Mudflap made trips to the truck by elevator and through the maze of halls to the parking garage. He stumbled upon an older fella lost in the maze, looking for the lobby. After all the help he had received in the last couple of days negotiating the area, it was his turn to guide this fella along the path. It was just a few steps out of Mudflap's way and he found it very rewarding to take the time to help.

MF.

MUDFLAP BLOOPER - From the chapter The Literary World

This segment were cut from the original tale.

An Unexpected Literary Snob.
and "A Blast from the Past" ! !

What makes a person's first reaction a "shoot down" when you're happy about something?

**If you really don't like their idea,
a thoughtful bit of feedback can be more productive.**

**You might also ask yourself,
What's their motive for telling you?**

Mudflap, Over and Out !

Note: This story may be considered inappropriate or distasteful. So, to spare my more refined readers, you may want to skip this section. I mark it in the beginning and end with a line of asterisks for your convenience.

****

Someone was mean about Mudflap's aspirations to be an author that he really didn't expect: one of his cousins who spent a lot of time with Mudflap and his family during the high school years.

When Mudflap finished his book and he got back from Washington D.C., he gave his cousin a call, excited to tell him

255

about it. He always looked up to his cousin, being one of the big kids when they were growing up. And he admired him for doing so very well working at a big newspaper.

Besides that, Mudflap's immediate family are all dead, and he has very few family left to turn to.

The Big Cousin was not at all impressed, not one bit. He said, "You can't just write a book, it takes at least a year or more." He didn't want to buy it, or read it. He was a real "Debbie Downer."

Well, Big Cousin wasn't that great of a guy. The Cousin was egotistical and could be a bully, too.

One night, back when Mudflap was just about to finish up his junior year of high school, he went out party-style with old "Big Cousin" and two other friends. Mudflap and friends were already bikers, (street and trail motorcycles) so they were conscious of bikes everywhere on the road.

They were flying down the very busy Washington Street in Middletown. Cousin was driving his Super Stock Dodge Demon. It was dark green with mag wheels, hood scoop, and a souped-up 340.

Cousin was showing off driving aggressively and hammering through intersections. Everyone was holding on tight. (Nobody in seatbelts.) A bike was pulling out. Mudflap and biker friend both simultaneously said, "Watch out for that bike!" Cousin snapped back very irritated, "Don't backseat drive me. Shut the ^%#@up." He hit the gas and sped through the next intersection.

They came down to where the Motor Vehicle Dept. was and were turning left towards Middlefield. A Harley was coming right straight at them. Cousin was obviously turning towards the bike.

Everyone wanted to warn him but nobody said anything, it was only a quarter mile since the last bike.

The three passengers just watched in silent horror as Cousin turned right into the Harley and hit him with a heavy, solid "SMASH!"

When they got out of the car, all were aghast as they saw the poor biker's left leg turned completely backwards against the way he was lying on the ground, like a broken doll. It was so messed up; it didn't look real.

That was only the beginning of the trouble. There was some kinda insurance problem or something. The biker was suing and coming after the Cousin. Here is really where the story gets bizarre.

Remember "The Crazy Man" from back in the old neighborhood? He had joined the Army and wanted to go to Vietnam, but instead he was stuck at boring Fort Devens in Massachusetts.

Cousin decided to split and head for Canada to escape the State and the biker's lawyer. And Craze, unable to go to war, decided instead to go AWOL from the Army.

With nothing better to do that summer, Mudflap joined them for the one-way ride.

They made their way up to Montreal but couldn't speak French so they kept going, living in the Dodge Demon and washing up in gas station bathrooms.

Craze had a Canadian ID and planned to start a new life. They pulled into a park off the highway for the night. Unable to sleep well in the car, Craze took a walk in the early morning and fell off a walking bridge. He ruptured his kidney and ended up in the hospital. There he found out quickly the Canadian ID he had bought was worthless. Unable to lie well, he spilled the beans and confessed to the authorities that he was AWOL.

Craze had a history of being accident prone, always gashing and tearing at himself. Once, during a hike in the woods behind the old neighborhood, Craze brought along his .22 pistol. He slid down an embankment, caught the hammer on the pistol, and shot himself in the leg.

Craze was a big husky guy. It took Mudflap and another big fellow to carry Craze out. As he lost more blood, he got weaker and heavier. They almost didn't get him out of there in time.

Now, he couldn't get a job and neither could the Cousin. They were running out of money fast.

Mudflap was the only one who found a job working as a short-order cook. Not really having the experience they required, (he had worked the prior summer at the scout camp kitchen), Mudflap was paid and fed well, but they had to let him go.

The three travelers, financed by Mudflap's pay, spent time in Ottawa and drove though Toronto, ending up back in the States. It what was like being in a crazy movie. They were broke in Buffalo where they hit rock bottom.

Ottawa is a beautiful city. Not being city boys, the three were very impressed with how nice and clean it was.

What a shock as they crossed back into the States and into Buffalo's filthy industrial area on the border.

They were just about completely out of money and, as it got dark, they wandered into the wildest place Mudflap had ever seen in his life.

Mudflap The Gloves Come Off

It was the summer of 1975. I hear today it's cleaned up, but they found themselves in the middle of the Red-Light District. To a country boy it was surreal, like a TV show. Everywhere there were decked out hookers, walking around, waving down, and approaching the cars.

It was quite the contrast from Ottawa. It sure would have been a lot more fun if they were not so broke and hungry.

Just when you think the trip couldn't get crazier, it did. Mudflap was down to his last few bucks and, having been the bread winner of the group, he was looking for some support from his much older friends. (Both Cousin and Craze had 4 to 5 years on him.)

They drove by a restaurant with an open wall of windows you could see right into. Obviously, it was a gay meeting place because it was packed with men only.

Jokingly, Mudflap said to his companions, "Hey, why don't one of you guys turn a trick and get us some food money."

Craze said, "I got a better idea," and, shockingly, pulled a pistol out of his backpack. It was the same .22 six-shot revolver he had shot himself with. You would think he would have learned to leave it home. He said, "Let's roll one of these guys."

Mudflap watched as his two companions shot fingers, two out of three, to see who would do the task of robbing a victim.

Cousin lost. Mudflap and Craze watched from the car as he went into the restaurant.

Mudflap was in shock as he watched him approach a table of guys. After a minute of talking with them, one got up and they both headed out the door.

259

Craze and Mudflap stared in disbelief as the cousin got into a car with this guy. He was no skinny, little feminine fellow; he was big and kinda scary looking. Mudflap said, "He's crazy. I wouldn't get in a car with that guy. I think Cousin is in over his head."

They waited there for what seemed a very long time and were getting worried that he might not come back at all. When, finally, he appeared, coming quickly towards the car, jumped in and fired up the Demon, pulling out fast.

Cousin was pretty jittery, and, of course, first thing Mud and Craze wanted to know was did he get any money? And what happened?

His story went something like: They went to park somewhere and the victim asked, "Do you blow?" The Cousin drew out the pistol and said, "Yeah, I'm going to blow you away."

Mud and Craze, of course, had to question the story. They razzed the cousin about maybe turning a trick instead, begging and crying for the money.

They were never sure how it really went down.

The gang left Buffalo and made their way across New York State, staying at youth hostels in Syracuse and Schenectady, where finally, The Crazy Man turned sane and went to a Western Union where he wired his parents for bus money to get home.

He went back to Fort Devens with his tail tucked and begging forgiveness. He left his pistol behind in case the cousin needed to turn another trick.

Mudflap and Cousin finally ended up in Albany, out of gas and penniless. In a somber mood, fed up, tired of being hungry and living on the road, Mudflap left his cousin, the Demon, and the pistol to their fate.

It was early on a Sunday morning, the city was quiet, the car was parked in front of some huge buildings. Cousin's head was hung low as Mudflap got out with his backpack, said, "Good-bye," and started walking home.

He was barely out of sight when the second car that went by stopped for Mudflap's thumb. He got a ride to the Interstate 90 on-ramp where he stood for only seconds before the next car stopped. The further away he got, the better it felt, until finally after weeks of hardship, the road was fun again.

Mudflap felt light. He had almost forgotten what it was like to be happy, he was weightless.

Later, he found out Cousin called his mommy for help, humiliated.

But I suppose it was better then turning tricks in Albany. Mudflap, Over and Out !

****

Well, the Big Cousin should have been nice.

MF.> Out !

Jay Alden Bailey

Author's Note

Despite all of Mudflap's troubles, he is really a happy guy. The worst years of being self- employed are behind him. That's the best part of being over sixty years old.

He is aware of the angry, middle aged/old white-guy crowd who feel the world is disenfranchising them; they should all get a grip on things.

Mudflap feels sorry only for the weak, abused, and disadvantaged people of our society.

He also cares about the environment with all its life forms and every breathing creature of the earth.

Everybody should pick a battle and become a Mudflap to someone or something, somewhere.

Big change starts small within us all.

Jay Alden Bailey, Over and Out !

Jay Alden Bailey

ACKNOWLEDGMENTS

Michelle Obama and her Quote:
"Bullies are scared people, hiding inside scary people."

From a lady who knows what it's like to be "thrown under the bus."

* * * * * *

Herman Melville

Pastor Martin Niemoller

Frank Zappa

Commander Cody and His Lost Planet Airmen

Jesus

Alfred Lord Tennyson

John Paul Jones

David Attenborough

Jacques Cousteau

Hermann Hesse

Aesop

Wayne Gretzky

And The Sensible Voice of Reason.

Questions and Answers from Mudflap's first Book

Q. Is everything in the book really completely true or are there some exaggerations?

A. Everything is 100% completely true with no embellishments at all. There are things left out. One can't throw everybody under the bus, there has to be somebody left to drive and be passengers.

I would like to take this opportunity to correct a detail which importantly keeps the first book 100 and 1% true. After the book was completed, I took a nostalgic trip to Durham and the old neighborhood. I stopped to visit my direct neighbor, the State Trooper, who never once ever complained in protest of the behavior going on at Mudflap's house.

Sadly, the Trooper has died but his widow was there. I told her about the book and said I was kind about her husband, complimenting his patience and respect of privacy he had displayed to his neighbors, and the fact that we never heard even a peep out of him in all those years.

But she had a correction that upon her reflection, Mudflap remembered it too. He didn't stop the parties. He didn't break up the fights, or he didn't care about the screaming and complete breach of peace. But he drew the line and came over in protest when Mudflap was shooting "real" full-sized arrows out of the second-floor window. That seemed to bother him.

As an adult, Mudflap gets it, but when reflecting on life during writing and being back there in the moment, it was so trivial compared to the complete chaos that was life back then, it completely escaped him at the time. So, all hats off again to my Trooper neighbor who showed there was, and is, a standard we all must conform to.

Q. What made you write the book?

A. The idea of what a Mudflap is and represents, and to obtain a copyright and trademark for that idea. Notice in the Introduction of this second book, I expand the term "Mudflap" as: A person who puts their own interest below that of another person or a "cause." Think of first responders and frontline workers, etc., etc., etc. Once you get the concept, it just keeps going on and on.

Q. In the original print (Unavailable at Amazon and stores) who was Mudflap's first love in the dedication? Was she his high school girlfriend?

A. Oh, God, no! Mudflap is way over her and glad he dodged that high velocity bullet. His first love was "The Little Girl from the Inn" who died early in life. Mudflap made that clear in the 2nd edition's dedication, reprinted for book stores.

Q. What happened to Bob Bailey?

A. He died broke, even trying to borrow money from his eldest son before the end.

At his last whirlwind dinner that he wanted to have with his sons, Mudflap did not attend. He didn't know his father was sick and was there to say goodbye. Bob Bailey brought a hunting rifle to the dinner that he was passing down to Mudflap from his grandfather. (Another great guy who left his family.) Brother gave it to Mudflap afterward, telling him how disappointed their father was that he didn't attend; the sharp teeth of Karma digging in deeply.

Q. Who's the Grand Inquisitor? Mentioned in only one line in the beginning of the chapter Bullies.

A. He was not one particular person: It's a reference to the Spanish Inquisition and The Catholic Church. It lasted three hundred and fifty years. He is more like the top sheriff of the county, the elected official in charge of all the other little sheriffs.

Mudflap had other issues he pointed at subtly in the first book like prejudice. My first focus was mainly: Parenting, Family, Guidance and Education, Business, Neighbors and Community.

I always joke, when selling books to my customers, that I stayed away from religion, politics, and my clients, but in *Mudflap II*, all bets are off.

Q. What happened to Mudflap's Son and Wife?
A. They moved an inconveniently, convenient distance away. In the absence of Mudflap's influence, they still experienced irritating drama to the extent of their inability to be happy and were soon divorced. When Mudflap questioned his son if he still blamed him for the problems they experienced, his reply was, "You were a trigger, but I realized that she just kept having more triggers, setting her off again and again in a relentless series of never-ending explosions." (Mudflap was just ahead of the curve and wasn't putting up with her crap.)
He now lives alone, out from under Mudflap's finances, the apron of his mom, and dictatorship of his wife.

He is residing, coincidentally and poetically perfectly, very close to Mark Twain's house in Hartford, completely independent at last.

Q. What's the difference between Mudflap's 1st and 2nd edition? And why a 2nd edition at all?
A. First of all, the shipping and handling is impossible for us to keep up with personally, so we can't be competitive in the national market. If you desire a 1st printed version (signed), or want a second print (signed), they are available on our website:
(www.mudflapthehero.com) and we will be happy to take the time to send you one.
Also:
The format in the 1st edition does not have a justified right margin required by the conventional system, as well as some other little layout, copyright, and cataloging issues. At first, I did not seek

advice at all from any editor or publisher, not wanting to give away my character idea before establishing the rights and trademark.

I took the opportunity to correct some typos that snuck through, as well as deleting a couple of phrases, a dozen to 14 repeating words and inserting about 30+ more comas, mostly around the word "too".

The cover has more elaborate art work and the write up on the cover is reduced to a minimum. I refer to the 2nd printed edition as "polished." This is the *Mudflap* version that's available on Amazon and the national market.

Jay Alden Bailey

Mudflap The Gloves Come Off

Jay Alden Bailey

MF.> Out !

Made in the USA
Middletown, DE
23 September 2022

10704931R00166